WHEN
POWER
MEETS
POTENTIAL

UNLOCKING GOD'S PURPOSE IN YOUR LIFE

T.D. JAKES

DESTINY IMAGE® PUBLISHERS, INC.

P.O. Box 310, Shippensburg, PA 17257-0310

"Promoting Inspired Lives."

This book and all other Destiny Image, Revival Press, MercyPlace, Fresh Bread, Destiny Image Fiction, and Treasure House books are available at Christian bookstores and distributors worldwide.

For a U.S. bookstore nearest you, call 1-800-722-6774.

For more information on foreign distributors, call 717-532-3040.

Reach us on the Internet: www.destinyimage.com.

ISBN 13 TP: 978-0-7684-0431-9

ISBN 13 Ebook: 978-0-7684-0432-6

For Worldwide Distribution, Printed in the U.S.A.

5 6 7 8 / 18 17 16 15

CONTENTS

Introduction 7

PART I   KNOW YOUR PURPOSE 11

CHAPTER 1   You Are on Purpose 13

CHAPTER 2   Get Ready for Your Moment 23

CHAPTER 3   Experience the God of Purpose 33

CHAPTER 4   Elevate Your Understanding of Purpose 45

CHAPTER 5   Find Your Place of Deposit 57

CHAPTER 6   Identifying Unrealized Potential 69

PART II   WHEN POWER MEETS POTENTIAL 79

CHAPTER 7   Unwrap the Gift of Exposure 81

CHAPTER 8   Recognize Your Moment 89

CHAPTER 9   Respond to Your Moment 99

CHAPTER 10   Seize Your Moment 109

CHAPTER 11   No Return to the Ordinary 121

CHAPTER 12   Make Firewood 133

CHAPTER 13   Live on a New Level 143

CHAPTER 14   The Final Tests 153

Conclusion 165

BONUS: Chapter 1 from *Power for Living* 167

INTRODUCTION

I am absolutely convinced that God is extending an unparalleled invitation to every believer at this unique moment in history. It's an invitation to step into your identity, embrace your destiny, and fulfill your purpose. For too long we've settled for too little. I've written this book to excite your mind and expose you to some radical new normals. The old normal isn't working if you currently define your life as purposeless and powerless. It is downright illegal for you, a child of God, to live this way when so much has been provided, and so much remains still untapped and available.

Make no mistake, new realms of power and anointing are not reserved for the super-spiritual or superlative saints—promotion is for everyone. God's eyes are not roaming throughout the earth, zeroing in exclusively on pastors, preachers, and evangelists. The Scriptures give us a different story.

> *For the eyes of the Lord range throughout the earth to strengthen those whose hearts are fully committed to him...* (2 Chronicles 16:9 NIV).

Consider this verse for just a moment. There is no mention of profession or placement; *only* posture of the heart. The Lord's eyes are searching for hearts fully committed to Him and His cause on the earth. These are the hearts that will fulfill purpose. When they are invited into a new level, people with hearts like this have what it takes to sustain that dimension of glory. These are the people who catch the gaze of God.

Will you catch His gaze? In this verse we also see a promise of power to those hearts that are fully committed to Him. Understanding this is vital. Your wholehearted devotion and commitment to God is what actually positions you for the divine moments that call forth your potential, strengthening and empowering you to fulfill your divine purpose.

I pray the following pages would remind you of the journey you began the moment you were born. In fact, your purpose preceded your coming into the world. Just as God called Jeremiah in the womb, He has called you in the same way.

Before I formed you in the womb I knew you; before you were born I sanctified you; I ordained you a prophet to the nations (Jeremiah 1:5).

Your journey began before birth. And now it's time for you to embrace it every day of your life. Apostle Paul gives us a glimpse of what this journey looks like, as he describes God's only desired travel plan for you—*from glory to glory* (see 2 Cor. 3:18). It's time for you to step into these new dimensions of glory, anointing, and power. It's time for you to recognize moments of divine visitation and run toward the supernatural promotion that's being presented your way. It's time for your potential to collide with God's power and release your purpose. That's what the world is waiting for—a people who actually step into their ordained assignment and fulfill their divine purpose.

> *You have untapped realms of ability, giftedness, and potential that are just waiting for one moment, one collision, one touch of God's power.*

You have untapped realms of ability, giftedness, and potential that are just waiting for one moment, one collision, one touch of God's power. Too many people are running around searching for purpose, when in fact purpose is wrapped up in their potential. When your potential is realized and released, your purpose can be fulfilled. I want to help position you for these moments that change everything.

This book is for anyone who is hungry to experience a shift. A change. A transition. Elevation. Promotion. What you've always known and how you've always done life is changing. There's a meeting scheduled. Power is on its way. Elijah's getting ready to throw a mantle on you. You won't be able to keep plowing the field after you've collided with a prophet. Your moment is at hand, and this moment changes everything.

While reading the pages ahead, ask the Spirit of God to lead and guide you. Invite Him to give you clarity. Elijah and Elisha are examples. Most likely, you're not a plower being called to be a prophet. We're simply mining the multi-dimensional principles that are observable in this story. This is not your handbook on how to be a doctor on a new level, or how to be a plumper at a new level, or how to be a school teacher on a new level, or how to be a lawyer on a new level. I can't share out of what I don't have.

You have a specific calling and purpose. I'm giving you basic principles that will prepare you to release your unique potential.

When you step into the new level, get the training. Pursue the instruction and teaching. Go after everything that will help you develop that potential. I'm here to coach you, equip you, prepare you, and arm you. I want to arm you, spiritually, to say "Yes" when power passes by. I want to sharpen your spiritual sight to recognize what is going on behind the *seen* and respond correctly on your day of visitation.

This book is all about the meeting of power and potential. I'll give you some glimpses of what this new level of living looks like, but my main goal is to help you work through the transition. When power comes, I want you to be ready. I want you to recognize your moment. Yes, there will be natural circumstances that set it up. But even more deeply and profoundly, I want to help tune you in to the spiritual dimensions of transition. You need to recognize what looks right, smells right, sounds right, and ultimately is your moment.

Above all, you must be ready to receive and run after the very touch that releases your potential: *God's power.*

PART I

KNOW YOUR PURPOSE

...Then Elijah passed by him and threw his mantle on him (1 Kings 19:19).

CHAPTER 1

YOU ARE ON PURPOSE

For You formed my inward parts; You covered me in my mother's womb. I will praise You, for I am fearfully and wonderfully made; marvelous are Your works, and that my soul knows very well. My frame was not hidden from You, when I was made in secret, and skillfully wrought in the lowest parts of the earth. Your eyes saw my substance, being yet unformed. And in Your book they all were written, the days fashioned for me, when as yet there were none of them (Psalm 139:13-16).

For we are God's masterpiece. He has created us anew in Christ Jesus, so we can do the good things he planned for us long ago (Ephesians 2:10 NLT).

"For I know the plans I have for you," says the Lord. "They are plans for good and not for disaster, to give you a future and a hope" (Jeremiah 29:11 ESV).

YOU HAVE A PURPOSE

Your hands have formed me and made me... (Job 10:8).

You have a purpose.

You were created *on purpose*.

You were formed, fashioned, and knit together by a skilled Craftsman, not some arbitrary cosmic explosion.

You are not an accident.

You are not an incident.

You are not a mistake.

You are not just a glob of protoplasmic material that is the result of a reckless night or a weekend between two passionate lovers.

You are not just a mere mixing together of DNA.

You have a divine purpose. You were allowed access into this dimension of life by the nod of the Creator Himself, that you would be strategically placed at this time, at this age, in your gender, in your ethnicity, with your gifting, and with your talent for God's divine purpose.

Even the wealthiest person on the planet could not offer up any suitable form of tender that could purchase *purpose*. Surely they wish purpose could have a dollar value assigned to it, because then the relentless nagging of their souls could be silenced. They could rest easy knowing that the one unknown of life has been secured. Purpose is priceless, while purposelessness is very costly.

You can live in this world and make all the money you could ever dream of and be as beautiful as you want and be as educated as you please and accomplish whatever you want to, but if you die without accomplishing your purpose, you are a failure, a reject and a fool.

THE ROOT OF PURPOSELESSNESS

The fool has said in his heart, "There is no God" (Psalm 14:1).

The fool has said, "There is no God, there is no purpose, there is no meaning." He further adds, "I can do my own thing, go my own way, live my own life."

The fool who says in his heart, "There is no God" has essentially said, "There is no purpose." To divorce one's perspective from the reality of a Creator, a Master Designer, and a Purpose-Author, one is rejecting purpose and meaning as a whole. This is no small statement because it is no small action. The repercussions of saying, *"There is no God"* are far-reaching into every arena of our lives and society. It is downright deadly to reject the reality of a Creator, for it is that very Creator who assigns value and purpose to the created. If the created is without a Creator, then who or what assigns value or purpose to the created? There are no constants. There's nothing certain. We are without anchors. No one knows who they are, because they are detached from the truth of *Whose* they are.

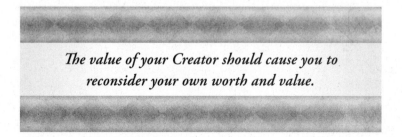

The value of your Creator should cause you to reconsider your own worth and value.

When Genesis 1 becomes a fairy tale and we are disconnected from the fact that we were created in the *"image and likeness of God,"* (see Gen. 1:26) that we were in fact hand-crafted in the image of the perfect Craftsman, purpose*less*ness abounds. Now, more than ever, we need this vision of the Creator and created; for as the Scripture says, *"Where there is no vision, the people perish"* (Prov. 29:18 KJV).

The world perishes because of the purposelessness of its people; people perish because they live without vision. I want to invite you to consider the vision of your Creator. As mentioned earlier, you are not some type of cosmic accident. You were hand-crafted and custom-made by a perfect Creator. The value of your Creator should cause you to reconsider your own worth and value. God did not make you in the image of an animal. He did not create you in the image of an angel. Rather, He created you in His very own image and His likeness. Time after time, Scripture invites us to consider the unlikeness of God.

> *Who is like You, O Lord, among the gods?...* (Exodus 15:11).

> *Lord God of Israel, there is no God in heaven or on earth like You...* (2 Chronicles 6:14).

> *Who is like the Lord our God, who dwells on high* (Psalm 113:5).

Because God radically stands out and above everything and everyone else in created order, consider the precious value that someone created in *His* image and likeness carries. *This someone is you.*

GOD CREATED YOU UNIQUELY

Then God said, "Let Us make man in Our image, according to Our likeness..." (Genesis 1:26).

Once you realize that you were created on purpose, and created in the image of the Creator, you begin to recognize that there are secrets stored up inside you. These are the very secrets that must be discovered and unleashed to a purposeless planet and a purposeless people.

There are secrets inside you that God has planted, secret talents and secret gifts and secret wisdoms that have been divinely orchestrated. These gifts, these talents, these abilities, these wisdoms, these solutions, these creativities—these are uniquely *yours*. God the Creator is multi-dimensional enough to create you uniquely. Trust His design. The moment you start to embrace how you have been formed and fashioned is the moment you step into the very purpose you were created for. God is not the author of prolonged purposelessness; you are. One of the most prevalent enemies to you stepping into your purpose is the downright deception that "the grass is greener." In other words, something in someone else causes you to reject, and ultimately neglect the unique purpose within you. This keeps you exactly where the enemy wants you, and sadly, where the world cannot afford to keep you. You cannot make a difference sitting off in a dark corner somewhere, wishing that you were someone else.

Stop, stop, stop wanting to be somebody else. Do not insult your Creator by insulting His creation. You were fearfully and wonderfully made. Can you even fathom what the psalmist is expressing by using those words—*fearfully and wonderfully?* (See Psalm 139:14.) You were created with awe. God didn't just throw you together, stand back and say, "This looks good." Because God fashioned you in His very image and likeness, He has a right to stand back and actually awe His own creation. Why? It's simply God standing in awe of His own handiwork; God awe-ing God. This is how He looks upon *you*.

In fact, God considers you a "masterpiece" (see Eph. 2:10 NLT). God made you the way He wanted to make you so He could use you at a particular time in a particular way; and if you start trying to be like somebody else, you're going to miss *your purpose.*

People don't miss their purpose and bypass destiny because God decides to take it away; they miss purpose because they fail to invest in *their* purpose. One of the greatest ways we fail to invest in what God has wired into our DNA is through rejecting who we have been uniquely created to be and what we have been created to bring to this moment in history.

YOU HAVE WHAT IT TAKES

His divine power has given to us all things that pertain to life and godliness... (2 Peter 1:3).

You have everything you need to do what you've been designed to do and be who you were created to be. I repeat, you have everything you need to accomplish your purpose. If God needed you to be tall, He would have made you tall. If He needed you to be better looking, He would have made you better looking. If He needed you to have a voice to sing, He would have given you a voice to sing. Everything about you was designed with intentionality. In fact, your design is directly connected to your purpose. If you neglect your design and refuse to celebrate *how* you were made, you will never step into *who* you were made to be. We have no right to question the Potter about how He fashioned and molded the clay.

In Romans 9:20 (NIV), Paul directly confronts this issue of questioning the Maker about how the creation was made. He writes,

But who are you, a human being, to talk back to God?
"Shall what is formed say to the one who formed it,
'Why did you make me like this?'"

God knew what He was doing when He created you like He did. He gave you the right IQ and He gave you the right personality. He gave you the right temperament. Do not despise your design, for the Designer made you a certain way so that you could accomplish a certain purpose. Like I said, the more you disregard your design and continue to want to be like someone else, the more you distance yourself from stepping into your created purpose. You, *as you are,* have got what it takes to *be* who God has created you to be. Yes, get educated. Yes, get equipped and trained. Yes, pursue knowledge, learning, and wisdom. Scripture tells us to pursue these things, as anybody can have as much of these things as he or she so desires. Just don't despise who God has created *you* to be.

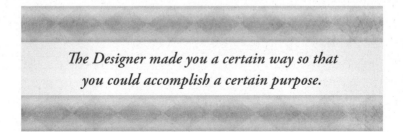

The Designer made you a certain way so that
you could accomplish a certain purpose.

Start believing this. You won't need as much counseling. You won't need as much therapy. You won't be as intimidated by other people. You won't be jealous of other people. If you understand your purpose, you will live in that purpose and you will discover your gifts and your talents and what you were put here to do.

Dealing with the Lie

Lead me by your truth and teach me, for you are the God who saves me. All day long I put my hope in you (Psalm 25:5 NLT).

And finally, whatever you've been through and whatever weaknesses you have, and whatever issues you've had—do not allow those weaknesses to abort your mission. Everyone's failed. Everyone messes up. Everyone's slipped, fallen, gotten up, fallen again, gotten up again, maybe wandered around in the dark for a season, moved on, etc. The devil is a liar, and he would love to deceive you right out of your destiny. One of the main tools he uses is reminding you of issues, hang-ups, setbacks, and sins. Your comeback should trump his lies *every* time. Your past is under the blood of Jesus. Your sins were dealt with at Calvary. God's not surprised by your weaknesses; this is why He promises strength! God's not caught off guard by your setbacks and problems.

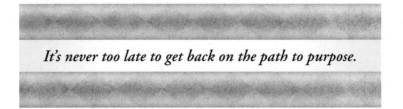

It's never too late to get back on the path to purpose.

Remember, it's not your weaknesses and failures that have the potential to abort your mission, it's how you see and respond to them. If you believe your weaknesses can abort your purpose, you will live in agreement with that lie. Nothing—absolutely nothing—can separate you from God's purpose for your life *unless* you start agreeing with lies. It's this type of agreement that causes you to veer off the path God has set for you. If you've been believing these lies, I encourage you to start disagreeing with the liar *today*. It's never too late to get back on the path to purpose.

I repeat—you have a divine mission to accomplish. You cannot allow *anything* to come between you and your purpose. In the pages ahead, we are going to look at the unique exchange that took place between Elijah and Elisha. As Elijah's time on earth was concluding, it was Elisha's turn to step up. If you need an example of someone who refused to let anything come between him and his purpose, this plowman-turned-prophet is your model. In fact, he is your mandate. I'm calling for a company of Elishas to rise up in this hour, recognize their moment of visitation, and start running toward the divine purpose God has ready to unleash to the world through their lives.

REFLECTIONS

1. In what ways is your design (how you were made) directly connected to fulfilling your purpose in life?

2. Why is it an insult to the Creator to question the way He made you?

3. How can your weaknesses and failures keep you from fulfilling your purpose?

Chapter 2

GET READY FOR YOUR MOMENT

So he departed from there, and found Elisha the son of Shaphat, who was plowing with twelve yoke of oxen before him... (1 Kings 19:19).

PREPARE FOR YOUR DESTINY-DEFINING MOMENT

Watch, stand fast in the faith, be brave, be strong (1 Corinthians 16:13).

Now we set out upon the journey to unlocking purpose. The first key to unlocking your purpose is preparing for destiny-defining moments. Be watchful, steadfast, and alert! It's in these moments when power meets potential, the power of God connects with the potential within you, and you are supernaturally catapulted into the pre-destined, preordained purpose that God has assigned to your life.

Throughout this book, we will be looking at the account of Elijah and Elisha and how their relationship is an example of what happens when power meets potential. For Elisha, it began with a *moment.* For you, it will be the same way. To step into our divine purpose, we need to recognize and steward our divine moments.

In this chapter, I want us to look at how Elisha responded to his moment of visitation. This gives us a powerful picture of how to respond when your moment walks up to you.

It begins in First Kings 19:19:

> *So he departed from there, and found Elisha the son of Shaphat, who was plowing with twelve yoke of oxen before him, and he was with the twelfth. Then Elijah passed by him and threw his mantle on him.*

Based on the text in First Kings 19, I want to share some vital keys to recognizing and stewarding your destiny-defining moments.

DESTINY-DEFINING MOMENTS HAPPEN QUICKLY

Then Elijah passed by him and threw his mantle on him (1 Kings 19:19b).

First of all, notice how quickly Elisha's moment happened. While Elisha was plowing, Elijah the prophet passed by, and *threw his mantle on him.* There was no ceremony or service. They did not sit down over a business lunch and discuss the logistics of what the mantle transference process would look and function like. There was no red tape. There were no emails. There were no phone conferences, Skype conversations, or cross-country travel reservations. Elisha was plowing, and Elijah—representative of Elisha's divine moment—*passed by him* and tossed the mantle upon him.

I know this example will probably mess up some people's thoughts. That's good. I want to mess you up, because it's in the process of messing you up when the Holy Spirit renews your mind. He's cleaning up your thinking and enabling you to accommodate His supernatural ways and workings. You see, I want to mess up your expectations of how you've got it planned out. So many of us are in bondage to preconceived ideas of how we assume God should launch us into our purpose and destiny. If your mind can comfortably wrap itself around a scenario, most likely, the Holy Spirit is going to uncomfortably remove the wrapping and invite you into an elevated perspective.

The main problem with our planning is that it discounts the power of moments—*quick moments.* Planning usually involves the image of a process. We consider the ideal process of how some certain result should come to pass. I say it again, God wants to radically mess up your process. This doesn't mean you stop thinking, cease dreaming, and quit planning. There is a difference between having a plan and being in bondage to your plan. Have a plan. Have a dream. Have goals. Have expectations. Have processes. Have a picture. Have an image. Have these things, but don't become yoked to them. Don't dare exalt your plan over the power of a God-ordained, destiny-defining moment. One divine moment orchestrated by the Master can shift things that have taken you a lifetime to try and change.

One divine moment orchestrated by the Master can shift things that have taken you a lifetime to try and change.

Going back to First Kings 19:19, it appears that Elisha's moment could have taken place in the blink of an eye. One moment he was plowing with twelve yoke of oxen; the next, he receives an invitation in the form of a mantle that would radically shift his destiny. The same is true for you. Your day of visitation is at hand. Your moment is waiting for you to be ready. Don't start getting paranoid, trying to figure out what your moment should look like. Elisha had no clue that his moment would look like some prophet throwing a mantle on him. In fact, it seems like Elisha recognized his moment, "after the fact." It was only after the mantle had fallen upon him and Elijah passed by that Elisha turned and ran after the prophet. Even if he was a minute behind his moment, he nevertheless recognized the power of his moment and responded appropriately.

Your key to being ready to run when your moment of visitation comes is simple. More than focusing on a moment, keep your eyes fixed on the Master. When the mantle hits, it is the still small voice of the Holy Spirit that will say, "This is your moment, son. This is your time, daughter. *Run after that prophet.*" We need to always be in a state of readiness and expectation, as we never know when those moments will happen when God's power collides with our potential.

DESTINY-DEFINING MOMENTS TAKE PLACE IN THE ORDINARY AND EVERYDAY

So he departed from there, and found Elisha the son of Shaphat, who was plowing with twelve yoke of oxen before him, and he was with the twelfth (1 Kings 19:19a).

Second, it is important to understand that destiny-defining moments take place in ordinary, everyday circumstances. In order to be trusted with a destiny-defining moment, we need to be good stewards of the unique moment we have been given *right now*.

Consider Elisha. He was simply being a good steward of where he was at his unique moment in history. He used his moments well, thus enabling him to be trusted with *the* moment. How we spend the sum of our everyday moments determines how we will respond to those life-altering, destiny-defining moments that come. I want to unpack this more, as I believe the secret to increase in the Kingdom has everything to do with stewarding what you have. How you handle the everyday shows God how you can be trusted with the extraordinary. Jesus notes this in His parable of the talents. The steward who was faithful receives this verbal recognition from his lord, *"Well done, good and faithful servant; you have been faithful over a few things, I will make you ruler over many things"* (Matt. 25:23). The "few things" for Elisha were his plowing. What are these "few things" for you?

> *How you handle the everyday shows God how you can be trusted with the extraordinary.*

When Elijah approached Elisha, the setting was nothing above average. There weren't heavenly beams and angelic choirs singing. Scripture tells us that Elisha was participating in something very common at the time. He was diligently plowing with the twelve yoke of oxen that were *before him*—the thing that was under his charge. He was faithful with what was before him, and this faithfulness positioned him to be in the right place at the right time when his moment came.

Too many of us want to chase after a destiny-defining moment; and as a result, we spend our entire lives running after something that should be running alongside us, ready to collide with our path. *Destiny-defining moments are like magnets to people who use their everyday moments well.* Do not despise where you are. Do not look negatively upon small beginnings. You are where you are for a reason, just like Elisha was exactly where he was for a reason—for that moment.

Also, too many desire a moment without recognizing that it is the sum of everyday moments that prepares a person to receive and run after their *moment.* Again, this should bring peace to our minds, which tend to fret over how and when our moment will come. This might sound backward, but the truth is those who become obsessed with seeking out *their moment* are actually ill-prepared for it and have the propensity to miss it when it presents itself. Why? God is looking for good stewards to trust with His greater works. He is looking for those who appropriately steward the lives they have been given before He promotes them into greater levels of glory, anointing, and power.

Many people seek after promotion from the usual, when in fact, God withholds the very thing they seek. He does not do this out of denial, but rather out of protection. Listen, God will protect you *from* your own promotion if that promotion has the potential to destroy you. If you're not ready for it. It's no mystery. Those who are faithful with the moments they have been given are positioning themselves for greater promotion; while those striving after promotion, but are neglecting the moments right in front of them, are being spared from a tragic downfall.

Keep in mind, it's everyday moments that prepare everyday people for extraordinary exploits. Character is developed in the moments. Integrity is cultivated in the moments. The fruit of the Spirit mature in the moments. Christlikeness, godliness, and holiness are birthed in the moments. God is examining your moments, for they gauge your preparedness for *the moment*.

DESTINY-DEFINING MOMENTS DEMAND A RAPID RESPONSE

And he left the oxen and ran after Elijah... (1 Kings 19:20).

The first thing we looked at was the swiftness of a moment's arrival. Scripture reminds us that *"Elijah passed by him* [Elisha] *and threw his mantle on him"* (1 Kings 19:19b). A quick moment demands an equally rapid response.

Before I continue, I want you to know that this is not some call to run after everything and make hasty decisions. There is balance. Elisha, no doubt, recognized that his moment was God-birthed and God-ordained. Before changing your life, switching jobs, moving across the country, marrying that guy, dating that girl, or doing something radical, the most important rapid, radical responses must always be to the One who authors your moment.

Let your heart be like Abraham's in Genesis 22, where he is brought into a destiny-defining moment. God instructs Abraham to sacrifice his son, Isaac, giving him up as a burnt offering before the Lord. Pay careful attention to how the scenario plays out. Before Abraham took his son up the mountain, prepared the altar, and yes, even raised the knife over the boy—only to be supernaturally stopped by the Angel of the Lord—Abraham offered a rapid response to God by saying "Yes" to His divine instruction. God set up the moment, and *"Abraham rose early in the morning and saddled his donkey, and took two of his young men with him, and Isaac his son; and he split the wood for the burnt offering, and arose and went to the place of which God had told him"* (Gen. 22:3).

Our rapid response always belongs to God first.

Our rapid response always belongs to God first. He will reveal the specifics. He will provide direction. His Spirit will lead us and guide us. In order to position ourselves for divine guidance, we must offer a rapid, definitive "Yes" to what God is asking of us. Abraham did not wait around, giving himself time to talk himself out of the difficult thing God was asking him to do. God gave Abraham instruction, and we notice that *"Abraham rose early in the morning"* to begin this journey. He didn't wait around, pacing the floor, giving himself the opportunity to consider some other, user-friendly options. First thing in the morning, Abraham got up and began walking toward a moment that would not only define his life, but a prophetic moment that would set humanity up for *the moment* that would change everything. That moment would be the Cross of Calvary.

How did Elisha respond to his destiny-defining moment? *"And he left the oxen and ran after Elijah"* (1 Kings 19:20).

Moments happen *that* fast. In future chapters, I want us to look at *why* these moments are so powerful and how they unlock the potential inside of you. For now, we know that any God-orchestrated moment is worthy of our rapid response. Our "Yes" to God prepares us to say "Yes" to every decision we need to make in order to embrace the moment that is being presented to us. Likewise, our "Yes" to God emboldens us to say "No" to everything that would try to restrain us from promotion. Previously, we considered people who were ill-prepared for promotion. Just as bad as those who receive promotion who are not prepared for it, are those who *are ready* for promotion, but don't recognize its life-changing invitation that demands their obedient response. Run after it like Elisha did.

When your moment arrives, all bets are off. Running after a moment cannot produce that divine moment in your life. However, responding to a moment, *when the moment presents itself,* will bring your life into alignment with the power of that moment, and ultimately, God's glorious purpose for your life.

REFLECTIONS

1. What do you think a destiny-defining moment looks like? What did it look like for Elisha?

2. What are the three characteristics of destiny-defining moments—and how should you respond to them?

3. What is the difference between running after a moment and responding to a moment?

CHAPTER 3

EXPERIENCE THE GOD OF PURPOSE

There he went into a cave and spent the night in that place; and behold, the word of the Lord came to him, and He said to him, "What are you doing here, Elijah?" (1 Kings 19:9)

And we know that all things work together for good to those who love God, to those who are the called according to His purpose (Romans 8:28).

For in him we live and move and have our being... (Acts 17:28 NIV).

KNOW THE GOD OF PURPOSE

In him we were also chosen, having been predestined according to the plan of him who works out everything in conformity with the purpose of his will (Ephesians 1:11 NIV).

It is by God's divine purpose that power and potential intersect and meet. It is a mystery that I think is worth discussing.

First things first. You need to know that the God you serve is a strategic God. He is the God of absolute purpose. He is the God who has a strategy, and according to Ephesians 1:11 (KJV), He *"worketh all things after the counsel of his own will."*

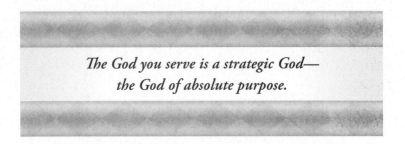

> *The God you serve is a strategic God—*
> *the God of absolute purpose.*

Nothing "just happened." Creation was not arbitrary. There are no cosmic blunders or mishaps. The God who created you is the same God who brought order to chaos, form to the formless, and purpose to nothingness. You may feel like that. You might feel like your life is formless, your future looks void of hope, and you have no purpose. Remind yourself, you were created by a God of Purpose. Nothing He made was created by accident—it was all sculpted with great skill and precision.

It was according to God's preordained purpose and divine design that He brought you into the world—and ultimately saved your soul. It was not your distress signal that brought God into your life. It was God who brought the distress signal that made you cry out after Him. Think about it. God is not just responding to your cry. He actually put the cry deep down inside you. He has put *eternity in your heart* (see Eccl. 3:11). He designed you in such a way that only He could satisfy the deep void inside your heart (see Ps. 42:7). In fact, the deep that *calls unto deep* was placed inside you by God Himself. He made it possible for you to even have a deep that could cry out to the deep of Himself.

God is not responding to you seeking Him. He put the seek down in you. This didn't just happen. You didn't just happen. God has a unique purpose and an essential role for you to play, and He's working everything, good or bad, in your life after the counsel of His own will. This should bring us great relief and freedom. Before we spend additional time studying how *our* potential is released and how we fulfill *our* purpose, it is foundational that we become acquainted with the God of Purpose. If we are confident in His nature as the One who is strategic and purposeful in all that He does, it will become much easier for us to trust that everything is in His most capable hands.

TRUST THE GOD OF PURPOSE

For the word of the Lord holds true, and we can trust everything he does (Psalm 33:4 NLT).

In view of this reality about God's purposeful character, we really ought to just stop the murmuring and complaining and sit back and let Him drive. Trust Him! His Word holds true, and everything He says, and everything He does can be trusted. He knows what He's doing. He will bring into your life who He wants to bring into your life. Conversely, He will bring out of your life who He wants to bring out of your life. He has a purpose and a strategy that defies human comprehension; and though many people don't understand why you are in the position or the role or the place you are in life, haters cannot stop your destiny. Their words, their slander, their accusations, their antagonisms, their doubts, their mockeries, their jokes—nothing any human being can say or do can restrain God's purpose from coming to pass in your life.

> *Nothing any human being can say or do can restrain God's purpose from coming to pass in your life.*

Consider the timeless accounts in Scripture of men and women persevering through their odds and experiencing their destinies. Mockers could not keep Noah from building an ark and saving the world. Egyptian armies could not keep Israel from leaving bondage and crossing the Red Sea. Insults could not keep Hannah from believing for her son. An insult-hurling giant could not keep David from securing a supernatural victory over the Philistine army. Persecution could not keep the Gospel of Jesus Christ from spreading throughout the known world. The seed of each monumental victory was everyday people trusting the God of Purpose in spite of what everything and everyone else was saying or doing.

Your job? Continue to agree with the God of Purpose. Remember, the enemy wants you to bow down to his lies. These lies come in the different forms we just looked at. He uses words. He uses memories. He uses something a parent said, something a teacher said, something a peer or student or co-worker said to try and deceive you right out of your destiny. Trust the God of Purpose, for the same God who is full of purpose is also full of power. He is also entirely sovereign. This means that He will make sure that your purpose is fulfilled, regardless what people say, regardless what problems come, and regardless how certain seasons of life treat you. Keep trusting the God of Purpose. The One who brings you *through* will also bring you *to*.

THE ENEMY OF YOUR PURPOSE

The thief comes only to steal and kill and destroy... (John 10:10 NIV).

Keep in mind, your purpose has an adversary (see 1 Pet. 5:8). This adversary, the devil, recruits a number of different methods of antagonism. These are the assignments aimed directly at your purpose. All of the mean things people have said, all of the mean things that they do, and all of the things that they set out against you are weapons of the adversary, targeted at your purpose. Stand on the truth that *"No weapon that is formed against thee shall prosper"* (Isa. 54:17 KJV). No weapon that the enemy aims at your purpose can dismantle it or defuse it. Why? Because God is going to see your purpose through unto completion. The One who *"began a good work in you will carry it on to completion until the day of Christ Jesus"* (Phil. 1:6 NIV). God's purpose for your life *will* come to pass.

> *No weapon that the enemy aims at your purpose can dismantle it or defuse it.*

Remember, satan is merely trying to steer you off course. He can't destroy your purpose. He also knows that you can't just lose your purpose, like someone loses a sock in the dryer or car keys in the sofa. He knows that his only formidable weapon against your purpose is securing your allegiance with his deception. When you start believing his lies over the truth of the God of Purpose, the devil beings to unleash his assault against your purpose. Again, it's not his tactics, tools, or terrorism that have any prevailing power against your purpose. What positions us for defeat is actually believing the enemy is more of a threat than he really is.

One of his main targets is your identity. He challenges your worthiness to fulfill God's purpose by using people to attack you. All of the lies, and the spirit behind the lies that are sent out against you, these are the enemy's attempts to distract you from purpose. The more you contemplate the negative things people are speaking against you, the less time you have to consider the greatness of the God of Purpose. He will surely bring His plans to fruition in your life and complete the good work He began. Your adversary knows that by getting people to spread lies and rumors and falsehoods about you, he is able to get you in that corner of distraction. It's like you are in the corner of a room, staring at a wall that is papered in lies. The lies try to consume your view, while God's truth is waiting just behind you, beckoning your re-focus.

If the enemy cannot distract you with lies, he will even try to use truth against you. He's desperate to distract you right out of stepping into your purpose by keeping your eyes off the God of Purpose. If you successfully stand your ground during his barrage of lies, the serpent will attempt another strategy. You see, the devil is an expert at digging up the dirt of your past and doing whatever he can to get you to stare at it—apart from the blood of Jesus. The Bible identifies satan as the *"accuser of our brethren"* (Rev. 12:10). You are his target, not God. He cannot accuse you before God because of the *"better things"* that Jesus' blood speaks (Heb. 12:24), but he knows that he can try to deceive believers right out of their status in Christ.

My goal here is not to make us overly conscious of the devil. Yet to defeat him and overcome his schemes, we must be aware of his tactics. Paul makes this clear, indicating that if we are ignorant of the enemy's devices, we can easily fall prey to his schemes (see 2 Cor. 2:11).

One of the enemy's greatest lies concerning your purpose is that *you are unworthy to step into so great of a purpose.* We just discussed the fact that he delights in trying to veer you off course by reminding you of your past, your sins, your setbacks, your failures, your issues, your obstacles, your bondages, your addictions, etc. Here's the truth—the God of Purpose will walk with you through each of these. He brings hope, healing, forgiveness, cleansing, deliverance, freedom—every solution to every obstacle. Listen to me, it's not the obstacle or the failure that keeps us from pursuing purpose, it's what we believe about the *power* of the obstacles that keep us in limbo. This is where the enemy works overtime, trying to convince us that our stuff has the ability to keep us from stepping into divine purpose. This is a flat out lie. Sin, hell, and death itself could not prevent Almighty God from reaching down into your mess, invading your life, cleansing you with Jesus' blood, filling you with the Holy Spirit, and setting you on a course for victory.

Just think about it, if the very power of death could not keep you from stepping into God's divine plan and design for your life, what could possibly hold you back? God has dealt with every possible barrier. However, there is one you will deal with throughout your life and you must learn to confront it appropriately should you desire to walk into your destiny. This is the boundary of belief. What do you believe about your purpose and your potential to fulfill it? Don't let the devil distract you with his lies and deception.

THE GOD OF PURPOSE USES YOU IN SPITE OF YOURSELF

And He said to me, "My grace is sufficient for you, for My strength is made perfect in weakness." Therefore most gladly I will rather boast in my infirmities, that the power of Christ may rest upon me (2 Corinthians 12:9).

We need to stop focusing on ourselves so much. God does not use us because of us; He uses us *in spite of us.* Paul the apostle recognized this on several dimensions. He had weaknesses that should have disqualified him from ministry. These were not restrictive, though. God used Paul in spite of his weakness, and He will use you in the same way. Remember, it is not because of you that God chose you; it is because of His divine purpose. Just think about it for a moment. Why in the world would God choose David to be a king? He had no background of a king, he was not trained as a king, he didn't live in the palace, was not reared up in an environment of kingly order. He was a shepherd boy. He was a goat chaser; and yet God said, *"I have found...a man after My own heart"* (see Acts 13:22).

Did that mean that David was perfect, or even close to being perfect? Absolutely not. And it doesn't just mean that David was a God-seeker, though he definitely fit that mold. Truly, God looked upon young David and declared, *I have found the man that is after My heart, that is after My purpose, that fits the spot of My purpose and destiny. I have found him. He's out there in the wilderness. He fits right into the strategic purpose of what I have orchestrated and I will use him in spite of himself.*

It is not because of you that God chose you;
it is because of His divine purpose

Now you can sit there, read these words, and act like you don't understand that, but if you have walked with God at all, you have come to discover that God uses you in spite of you—not because of you! In fact, the conditions that seem to make you the least likely candidate for a God-sized destiny are the very factors that maintain your humility.

The devil is trying to use our own weapons against us. We need to know that our past is not a weapon against us, but an anchor—a pillar. Our past, our surroundings, and our upbringing reminds us where we came from, that God stepped in and chose us in spite of ourselves.

Once when I was being interviewed, the reporter noted that I exhibited a humility that did not match my circumstances, and then proceeded to ask me, "How do you stay humble, Bishop Jakes?" Here's my answer. I said, "Because I know me. I have no choice but to be humble. It is by God's grace that I stand where I stand. He uses me in spite of me. There are things that pulled me out of my comfort zone, that pulled me out of my insecurities and out of my inhibitions. *He* pulled me. I had no choice but to come. I didn't come because I was wonderful or better or perfect or superior or anything else. I came because He drew me by His right hand. He stretched forth His hand and said, *'I call you unto Myself, and I'm going to use you right there.'*" And the same is true for you!

Your Piece in the Puzzle

Though the Lord is great, he cares for the humble...
(Psalm 138:6 NLT).

You will never find your place until you find your purpose and you understand how we all fit together in the grand scheme of things. Remember, God is the One who assigns your greater significance. You may not see it. You may not comprehend it. It might not compute with your natural mind, but you have to trust the God of Purpose. He has a master plan to assemble the pieces together in such a way that from His divine vantage point everything fits together, everything makes sense, and there is a perfect image of all the parts working together as a whole. I repeat, in order to embrace the greater significance, you must trust the God of Purpose and not attempt try to do His work for Him. He is the only One capable of putting this great jigsaw puzzle of purpose together. In order to fit in, you need to humble yourself before His purpose.

Think of it this way. Everything fits together like a jigsaw puzzle. Have you ever tried to sit down and put one of those things together? I'm not good at those puzzles because I don't have the patience. It takes order. It takes time. It takes meticulous observation and precision on behalf of the assembler to fit one like-piece with its corresponding part.

With me, I want the stuff to fall into place *when I say so.* And so when I start working with those puzzles, I get angry. I get mad because there are too many of those little bitty pieces.

You know how it goes when you are trying to put one of those things together. One of the pieces either fell down behind the couch and you can't find it, or someone walked off with one in a pocket, and the entire project goes on hold because of the gaping hole in the puzzle.

I get no joy out of putting puzzles together. The process gets on my nerves. My patience is not suitable for the puzzle process. Because of this, I try to improvise. This is where so many of us stray from safety when it comes to walking down the path of purpose. We step into uncertain territory because of our unwillingness to wait on the Master Builder's divine timing and precision, and we start trying to make things fit together.

You know you've tried it. When one of those puzzles gets on my nerves and I can't find the missing piece—or the right piece—I'll take a piece that's *close* to fitting and I'll try to jam it down into the spot because it's so close to fitting. But it doesn't work out. Even though it looks very similar to the right piece, it is still the wrong piece. In trying to make a wrong piece fit, you have to tear out something to make it become something that it is not in order to fit into the place that it really doesn't fit. Did you catch that? You need to celebrate who the Master Craftsman has created you to be, and not try to distort or disfigure yourself in trying to bring your purpose to pass the way *you* assume it should take place. Yes, there are growth areas. Of course we learn, grow, change, and develop. I'm not talking about that. I'm talking about who you are as the integral piece to God's glorious puzzle. I'm talking about how you have been uniquely designed, intricately wired, and purposefully positioned. Don't try to become someone else in order to fulfill your purpose. Why? As long as you strive to be someone you're not, you will never fulfill *your* purpose.

> *As long as you strive to be someone you're not, you will never fulfill your purpose.*

Remember, when you attempt to malign God's design by fitting yourself into a scheme or scenario where you don't fit, you have to tear something in who you are. What happens when you tear, or change yourself, to try and become someone else in hopes of trying to fit somewhere that you don't actually belong? Your little plan actually messes up the bigger picture of what you're trying to do, which is ultimately fulfill purpose. I repeat, the longer you tear yourself by trying to become someone else, the longer you will prolong your journey toward purpose. God curved you where you needed to be curved, made you straight where you needed to be straight, made you blue where you needed to be blue, yellow where you needed to be yellow, and as soon as you find and celebrate that place where you fit...*purpose happens.*

REFLECTIONS

1. How does the enemy try to distract you from fulfilling your purpose?

2. What does it mean that God uses you in spite of yourself?

3. What can happen if you try to bring your purpose to pass yourself instead of waiting on God's divine timing?

CHAPTER 4

ELEVATE YOUR UNDERSTANDING OF PURPOSE

Now when David had served God's purpose in his own generation, he fell asleep; he was buried with his ancestors and his body decayed (Acts 13:36 NIV).

One generation shall praise Your works to another, and shall declare Your mighty acts (Psalm 145:4).

YOUR POSITION IN GOD'S DIVINE PROCESS

But let him who glories glory in this, that he understands and knows Me... (Jeremiah 9:24).

Once we recognize that God is orchestrating a master jigsaw puzzle, we begin to live our lives very differently. Why? Because no moment is arbitrary. Randomness is not part of the equation. We don't just wake up to sleepwalk through our day, only to come home, go to bed, wake up and start the process all over again. God is elevating your perspective concerning your purpose, for there are seeds of fulfilling your purpose in every waking moment of your life. With every moment comes greater understanding of your unfolding purpose. You walk with a speaking God. This is your glory—that you know Him, and yes, understand His unfolding plan of piecing the puzzle together. I want us to study the process through which God begins putting the puzzle together. This intersection is where power collides with potential and pushes us toward purpose.

First, understand that there is a divine process for putting the puzzle together.

> *In the beginning was the Word, and the Word was with God, and the Word was God. He was in the beginning with God* (John 1:1-2).

The Word is the logos. In the beginning, we see that the logos was with God, and the logos was God. The logos in the beginning was the strategy, and the strategy was with God and the strategy was God, and on account of His divine strategy, He pulls you in to fit a particular place and time and destiny. He then calls you to meet who you need to meet right when you need to meet them to draw the picture, and start assembling the jigsaw puzzle of His purpose in the earth. Our God is the Master Strategist. Everything He does brims with intentionality. God is not the author of coincidence; He is the sculptor of divine providence.

God is not the author of coincidence; He is the sculptor of divine providence.

You must keep your eyes on God's divine strategy. If you don't, you run the risk of adopting the Elijah perspective. Even though we are studying the transference that took place between Elijah and *Elisha,* during Elijah's final golden days on earth, this prophet of power experienced some deep moments of despair. Why? He redirected his vision away from his purpose.

THE GREATER PICTURE OF PURPOSE

But he himself went a day's journey into the wilderness, and came and sat down under a broom tree. And he prayed that he might die, and said, "It is enough! Now, Lord, take my life, for I am no better than my fathers!" (1 Kings 19:4)

Why did Elijah want to die here? Because something was missing, and he could not figure out what it was. His pain starts pointing him toward his purpose. At this point in the story, he has gone as far as he can go without meeting Elisha. It is in this same chapter, First Kings 19, where Elijah experiences some of his darkest moments, as well as his finest hour. One would think that the prophet's finest hour preceded this chapter, when he called down fire from Heaven, experienced a miraculous demonstration of the power of God, and executed the false prophets of Baal. God used him to dramatically impact the spiritual landscape of an entire region, all in a single scene. And yet in the following chapter, we see the same man who experienced an overwhelming victory suffer under overwhelming depression. How was this possible?

As incredible as the victory at Mount Carmel was, that was not the moment where power would meet potential. Don't be deceived. Some moments that appear the most suited for purpose can actually distract you from fulfilling your purpose. Don't settle on a high. Celebrate breakthrough and victory, but don't mistakenly assume that a single demonstration of God's power *is* your purpose coming to pass. Rather, it serves as a landmark on your road to fulfilling your ultimate purpose.

> *Some moments that appear the most suited for purpose can actually distract you from fulfilling your purpose.*

There was a greater picture of purpose in Elijah's life than simply experiencing a significant victory against the prophets of Baal on Mount Carmel. It would have been easy for Elijah to mistakenly assume that a victory of that size was, in fact, the fulfillment of his purpose on earth. Perhaps he did entertain such a thought process. However, when we settle for small when God has greater, the ache and groan in our spirits will begin to push us outside of our wildernesses.

Elijah was not only in a wilderness physically, he was also in a wilderness mentally. Elijah's life purpose was not fulfilled in simply calling down fire from Heaven and destroying the false prophets of Baal. Likewise, your purpose is not fulfilled through some notable exploit you perform, a mighty act, or some type of spectacular feat. Even though these are God-ordained and God-orchestrated, they are moments that ultimately fade. Displays of power are fleeting, but transferences of power *awaken* potential in others. This is what Elijah was waiting for; he just didn't see it at the time.

Remember, God's vantage point includes so much more than human eyes are capable of capturing. It's tempting to coast on yesterday's victory, when in fact, God has bigger prepared. He is the God of *Greater Works*. I repeat, God has better. His vision is not for something fleeting or forgettable, but rather something sustained and supernatural. This is what He was preparing Elijah for, and yes, even used some of the prophet's pain to position him to anoint his successor, Elisha.

THE MULTI-DIMENSIONAL NATURE OF YOUR PURPOSE

"For My thoughts are not your thoughts, nor are your ways My ways," says the Lord (Isaiah 55:8).

Your Mount Carmel victory should not be un-scalable. Why? Because your purpose is not wrapped up in a single event; rather, it's your active participation in an unfolding, lifelong process. There are landmarks along the journey, but we cannot confuse a landmark with ultimate fulfillment. Perhaps Elijah considered his fiery victory as ultimate purpose-fulfillment, when in fact, it was a piece of Heaven's divine jigsaw puzzle for his life and overall contribution to God's purpose in the Earth. Our problem is that we often mistake great victories for the entire puzzle, and then become disappointed when another major victory is not soon waiting in the wings to continue that momentum.

We start redefining our purpose, not by the divine orchestration of God's unfolding plan, but rather by the size and scope of our victories, miracles, and blessings. Remember, these are all integral, essential parts of the journey. However, when we assume that *part* of the journey has become the *whole* journey, we position ourselves to live perpetually disappointed. The very object of our purpose is reduced to something that happened in the past. Right after your breakthrough comes and right on the other side of your miracle, is an ominous future.

Consider it for a moment. What happens when we believe that our best days and greatest victories are behind us, not before us? We cease pushing forward, for we see no potential in forward momentum. That's the danger of believing that purpose is fulfilled in an event or a landmark moment. There is far more to your purpose on earth than one breakthrough or miracle, no matter how spectacular or significant it appears to be.

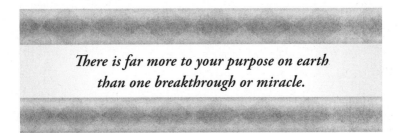

There is far more to your purpose on earth
than one breakthrough or miracle.

It's like believing that a piece of the puzzle is the entire puzzle. And yet, God is in His mercy gives us vision to see that the puzzle piece has interconnected edges longing for a complement. And you know that complement longs for a complementary piece, and so on and so forth. This is why I believe the puzzle analogy is most helpful in recognizing the flow and unfolding of God's purpose in our lives.

In other words, if we assume that a single victory or a significant event in our lives marks the complete fulfillment of our divine purpose, God is quick to remind us that what we assume is the whole is only a part. An essential part, yes, but still only a part. He gives us eyes to see the protruding edges on the pieces that are meant to connect and link with other pieces. He gives us the ability to see that what we perceive to be the be-all and end-all actually has missing portions. You know how a puzzle piece has missing ends and edges, purposed to be complemented by a corresponding piece? In the same way, your breakthrough has missing portions. Whatever it is—a breakthrough, a blessing, a miracle, a victory, a promotion, an increase—God's purpose is higher and bigger. One event is merely one piece of your puzzle of purpose. One victory helps complete the puzzle, but is inadequate to masquerade as the entire image.

Make no mistake, events launch us into purpose. Breakthroughs escort us from one level to the next. Miracles override natural law, and position us in places that we could not have gotten to by ourselves. We celebrate moments without mistaking them for the ultimate masterpiece of God's divine design. We steward every significant event that takes place as a push that takes us from one dimension to the next, one realm of glory to another. We don't camp out at Carmel. We don't build a memorial to every miracle—even the outstanding ones. Even the ones where fire falls down. We don't pitch a tent and try to live in yesterday, when in fact today is standing before us and we gaze, without purpose, into an uncertain future. Instead, we must see the catalysts for what they are and embrace their ability to move us along God's route for our lives.

THE MULTI-GENERATIONAL NATURE OF YOUR PURPOSE

For I will pour water on him who is thirsty, and floods on the dry ground; I will pour My Spirit on your descendants, and My blessing on your offspring (Isaiah 44:3).

In the same way assuming that a single significant event could capture the fulfillment of our purpose, we severely limit the expression of purpose when we simply focus on one person or a single generation. Purpose is beyond you, and it is beyond me. It is beyond our big breaks. It is beyond our successes. It is beyond our breakthroughs. It is beyond our victories. In the same way that purpose was beyond Elijah, so the expression and fulfillment of purpose is beyond a single generation. When you collide with God's power, the object of transformation is not just *you*. Even though you are being hit, and you are being marked, and your potential is being awakened, you step into the flow of something that was going on before you stepped onto the scene—and will continue when you are gone. He is the God who pours out His Spirit on *descendants* and *offspring*.

We miss the mark when we inappropriately elevate a single individual to a place of memorial without recognizing the *role* the person played in the continuing fulfillment of the purpose he or she served. We serve purpose, because we serve God. Remember, God is the God of Purpose. We are here to serve His purpose, not the other way around. Consider King David. Scripture tells us that he *"had served God's purpose in his own generation"* (Acts 13:36 NIV). Even the phrase, "served a purpose," carries the connotation that a purpose is beyond us. Purpose does not serve us; we serve it. We cater to it. We revolve our lives around purpose. We don't place demands on purpose. We don't dictate to purpose. Instead, we let it dictate to us and as we serve God's purpose in our own generation, we play a vital part in the great unfolding agenda of God. You serve a multi-generational God. He is God of Abraham, Isaac, and Jacob.

In serving God's purpose, we submit to His plan. Serving a purpose is not our invitation to celebrity status; serving a purpose is the call to lay everything at the feet of Jesus and say, "I'm in the King's service." The moment we take our eyes off the greater purpose of God and its multi-generational impact, we run into two dangers: 1) inappropriate focus on humanity, and 2) hindering the generational continuance of God's purposes.

When we take our eyes off the multi-generational nature of our purpose, we can mislead ourselves into believing that *we* are solely responsible for bringing our purpose to pass. This is both overwhelming and arrogance-producing. It's overwhelming to believe that saving the entire world is on our shoulders, but it is likewise arrogance-producing to assume that *we* have the ability to bring such a God-sized purpose to pass by ourselves. We must be careful to always see ourselves in the context of the greater picture, the larger puzzle. Each person is an interconnected piece, linked to other generations. When someone is divorced from his or her rightful place in the unfolding of a purpose, the person becomes elevated beyond appropriateness. The piece ends up receiving perverted recognition, for it is really the completed puzzle that solved the problem. The problem was incompletion; the process produced completion.

The process is beyond you, and it's beyond me. The process involves generations locking pieces to complete the puzzle. At one point, there was a puzzle that was missing pieces. However, as more and more pieces took their place in the puzzle, the purpose came to pass and was ultimately fulfilled. But think of how ridiculous it would be to assume that one piece, in and of itself, sufficiently completed the puzzle. This would be believing a lie and living in delusion. We play integral, interconnected parts in completing the most glorious puzzle conceivable—the puzzle of God's purpose being fulfilled in the earth.

> *You play an integral, interconnected part in completing the most glorious puzzle conceivable!*

God's great puzzle of purpose highlights two primary methods of interconnectedness between pieces. First, we are interconnected with each other in our present generation, recognizing what gifts, talents, abilities, and resources other people bring to the table in complementing who we are, and likewise what we bring complementing who they are. Second, we recognize how our generation is vitally interconnected with future generations. In Psalm 145:4, we are given one of many examples throughout Scripture revealing God's vision for interconnecting generations.

This was God's purpose in colliding Elijah with Elisha. The puzzle did not conclude with Elijah. It would be tempting to gaze through the annals of history and fix our eyes on this man of power for his hour. Many of us do, in fact. We look at the life of someone God used powerfully and place an unhealthy amount of emphasis on *that one person,* when in fact we should be looking into his or her *purpose.* The purpose did not begin with that one person, and it does not end with that one person. While we honor the call of God upon someone, we must take it a step further and decipher the piece of the puzzle he or she served as in that generation. Why? This gives us clues to how the purpose will continue to unfold.

God's ministry of breakthrough, power, miracles, and cultural-transformation did not conclude with Elijah; if anything, it increased in momentum when the mantle hit Elisha. The same is true for the work of God in this hour, in your life. If you wish to take your place as a carrier of God's purpose, you must recognize that purpose goes beyond yourself and beyond your generation.

REFLECTIONS

1. What is the "greater picture" of God's purpose for your life?

2. How does your purpose have many different dimensions?

3. Describe how you understand purpose to be multi-generational.

CHAPTER 5

FIND YOUR PLACE OF DEPOSIT

So Elijah went and found Elisha son of Shaphat plowing a field... (1 Kings 19:19 NLT).

MEETING THE CRITERIA FOR CARRYING PURPOSE

We just explored how purpose is much bigger than you might have imagined. In the same way that purpose did not start with us, it does not conclude with us. It is multi-generational. We briefly looked at the example of King David, who *"had served God's purpose in his own generation"* (Acts 13:36 NIV). He recognized that purpose was bigger than his own piece of the puzzle, and simply served his uniquely assigned moment in history. Result? King David's life continued a momentum that ultimately birthed the Son of David, *Jesus Christ.*

In the same manner, Elijah sought to sow into a successor who would continue to carry his divinely assigned purpose. Going back in the story to where Elijah is discouraged after his Mount Carmel victory, the Lord informs him, *"I have reserved seven thousand in Israel, all whose knees have not bowed to Baal, and every mouth that has not kissed him"* (1 Kings 19:18). He was looking for soil to sow into, ready and fertile for the perpetuation of purpose.

In the following chapters we are going to switch gears and examine the process from Elisha's viewpoint. However, it is important to note the principle here. Elijah was searching for a place of deposit and could find none. He had a mantle. He had experience. He had wisdom. He had revelation. Elijah had so much to impart, so much to release, but it was reserved for specific ground.

Elijah's mantle was custom-sized for Elisha. Whether or not this is true in the literal sense, Elisha was the only one capable of wearing that mantle, for he was the designated place of deposit. The person of deposit is able to don the mantle. You see, none of the people Elijah had encountered or interacted with, up to this point, had met the criteria for the release of what he wanted to impart. Even though there were seven thousand in Israel who had not prostituted themselves with false gods, there was only one man suitable to be Elijah's spiritual successor. *Elisha* was Elijah's place of divine deposit. This is something we must learn to recognize if we are going to step into our purpose.

Don't waste your time trying to sow into unresponsive ground. It's got to be fertile. Listen, there is definitely a time for you to dig in, have resolve, and refuse to back up or back down. In these cases, your sowing is the very element God wants to use to supernaturally break up the fallowed ground (see Hos. 10:12). You need to exercise discernment, and evaluate whether or not the ground is worthy of your seed. What is your seed? It's your time. Your effort. Your passion. Your sweat. Your tears. Your intercessions. Your contending. Your laboring. When it comes time for you to sow and invest into someone else, identifying that person as a potential carrier and perpetuator of the purpose on your life, ensure that he or she is a suitable resting place for the deposit you carry. Otherwise frustration will overwhelm the process.

Likewise, you need to prepare *your* heart to be fertile ground for what power wants to impart. You really need to grasp both sides of this principle. Most of this book will focus on Elisha, and in turn, place you in the Elisha position. Elisha is the one being pushed into his purpose; in the same way, I believe God wants to set you up for those meetings with power that unlock your potential and set you on a whole new course.

For the sake of this book, you are Elisha. Got it? You are the one God wants to impart power into that will unlock potential. With that in mind, it's key to first study how Elijah chose a successor to sow into. This shows us *who* God is looking for to collide with His power.

THE PRACTICAL SIDE OF SOWING

And he who reaps receives wages, and gathers fruit for eternal life, that both he who sows and he who reaps may rejoice together (John 4:36).

Before we explore this principle any further, I want you to identify just how relatable it is to your life. I don't assume every person on the planet is a vagabond prophet like Elijah who just recently called fire down from Heaven. However, Elijah was a man marked by purpose. God had a purpose for Elijah in his generation prepared before the foundation of the world. In the same way, the God of Elijah has marked you with purpose. He has fashioned you for destiny. We reviewed this in the opening pages of this book. You're not a cosmic accident; you are the intricate handiwork of the God of Purpose. You have been placed in this moment, at this hour, in this season of history to fulfill your purpose in *your generation,* just as King David did.

What does this look like for the businessperson? The stay-at-home parent? The plumber? The accountant? The doctor? The coffee shop barista? The college student? The banker? Regardless what you are doing in life right now, you have been called to fulfill your purpose in your generation. Likewise, part of fulfilling your purpose is making an investment in other people and being one who is investable.

In the chapters to come, we are going to examine what it looks like for you to intersect with God's power, and how this power actually draws out your potential. This was exactly what happened between Elijah and Elisha—Elisha's potential was awakened and released when he collided with the power on Elijah's life and received Elijah's mantle.

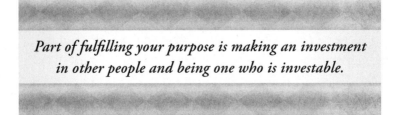

Part of fulfilling your purpose is making an investment in other people and being one who is investable.

I want you to have eyes opened for the divine collisions in your life—not only for those who collide with you, but keep your eyes open to the people God brings into your life to collide with. You have something to release, and you have something to receive. Yes, you. I don't care what you're doing right now. I don't care if you are a multi-millionaire or some broke college student living off noodles and peanut butter. Purpose is beyond your socio-economic status. Purpose is not thwarted by the kind of house you currently live in. Purpose is not intimidated by your situation or circumstance. If you are a child of God, you carry the power of God—and that supernatural power awakens potential. You carry this power, and at any moment this same power can collide with you and unlock possibilities that your mind cannot even fathom. All it takes is a single moment. One encounter. A single meeting.

The key is sowing where your contribution is valued and appreciated. Right now, the context is making investment in others. There will be times and places where what you bring is not appreciated, but it is something you *must do*. We can't go through life waiting to be appreciated before we do the right thing. That is not what I am talking about here.

Our context is mentorship. We're talking about the people you make an investment in and pour your life into. It's about being on the lookout for those who carry your DNA. Sure they might look differently, talk differently, act differently, smell differently, and dress differently. None of those externals matter when you see potential in that person. These are the people and environments where you are called to invest your pearls—the time, ability, gifting, talent, and wisdom of most precious value.

In the same way, I encourage you to be ready. Power is out there looking for you. Sowers are seeking those who carry the same DNA, same heartbeat, and same vision. You may look different, but that doesn't matter. If you are seed-ready ground, power is going to hit and awaken everything inside of you that needs to come out.

How to Identify "Seed-Ready" Ground

For he who sows to his flesh will of the flesh reap corruption, but he who sows to the Spirit will of the Spirit reap everlasting life (Galatians 6:8).

Keep in mind, you cannot give your pearls to pigs (see Matt. 7:6). No matter how tired you are of carrying them, no matter how much you're ready to release them, you cannot take the things of God and give them to people who are not ready. Wait and be looking for seed-ready ground. What does this look like?

One of the key characteristics is a lifestyle of one who frequently sows *to the Spirit* (see Gal. 6:8). Their lifestyle is marked by consistent spiritual investment. They are close with God—and you can see it. You see the fruit of their investment. Not everyone walks in this dimension, because not everyone stewards the seed he or she has received in the Spirit.

Think of all the believers out there. Yes, they are born again. Yes, they are washed in the blood. Yes, they have the Holy Ghost living inside them. Do you know how many people have this beyond-priceless inheritance living inside them, and yet live like spiritual paupers? They live in spiritual poverty because they sow to the flesh. Their spirit was transformed when they were born again, but they still live like the world lives. They still operate and think and respond and behave like everyone else. Something happened in the core of their being, *but*, hear me, they are not sowing into it. They are not stewarding the seed of God in their own lives.

God planted a seed in their spirit when you came to Christ. That's the seed of His Spirit—the Holy Spirit. He's not looking to simply hang out, unbothered, in our spirits for 70, 80,

90, or 100 years. The Holy Spirit is a Person looking for cooperation. He's seeking ones who desire total divine invasion of
every realm of life. He's waiting for the ones who will sow into
the Spirit and reap for themselves transformed minds, healed
emotions, and God-ward wills. The ground must be spiritually
ready. Are you?

Remember when Moses came down off the mountaintop
with glory beams shooting out of his face (see Exod. 34:29-
35)? He was ready to impart something to an Israel that was
not ready. They were sowing into the flesh. They received this
glorious invitation from Jehovah, and what were they doing?
Impatience brought them to idolatry. Moses comes down and
finds them dancing naked around the golden calf and actually
has to cover the glory that he was ready to release. Why? The
people were not ready to receive on the level that he was ready
to release. Do you see the parallel? For the power inside of you
to release the potential in someone else, there must be a readiness on their end.

> *Don't be caught dancing before the golden
> calf during your season of visitation.*

In the same way, for the power upon someone else to awaken
your potential, you must be ready. For you to step into the things
that God has purposed for your life, you must be prepared and
seed-ready ground. You must be ready in season and out of
season. Don't be caught dancing before the golden calf during

your season of visitation. Too many believers give up just before their moment, either because they cannot find fertile ground to release impartation, or because they have been patiently waiting to receive the mantle of Elisha and are losing heart. They are waiting for Moses to come down off the mountain—and are getting impatient.

I encourage you to be ready for your day of visitation. Be faithful. Continue plowing where God has you plowing right now. You don't know what it will look like, sound like, feel like, or smell like when power comes. God's orchestration is perfect, and it is sovereign. Your supernatural setup will come in His divine timing. Those catalysts that catapult you further and further into your purpose by awakening greater dimensions of untapped potential—they cannot be setup by our scheming. They cannot be initiated by our own human devices. In fact, when we insert ourselves into the process, we start tearing up the puzzle pieces.

Think of the other examples in Scripture. Jesus came onto the scene and said, *"I still have many things to say to you, but you cannot bear them now"* (John 16:12). There were certain realities that Jesus restrained Himself from sharing with the disciples because the soil was not yet ready for the impartation. It would only be ripe and ready upon the coming of the Holy Spirit.

WHEN THE STUDENT IS READY, THE TEACHER WILL APPEAR

And let us not grow weary while doing good, for in due season we shall reap if we do not lose heart (Galatians 6:9).

When the student is ready, the teacher will appear. This was certainly true for Elijah and Elisha, and it is likewise true for your life. You have to be ready to receive on the next level and others have to be ready for your next level of impartation. By now you have probably noticed that all of us wear both hats at some point—teacher and student, Elijah and Elisha. All the while you are receiving from the teacher, you are releasing to students. All the while you are receiving as a student, you are releasing as a teacher. This is the process that Jesus described, *"Freely you have received, freely give"* (Matt. 10:8). As you receive more, more is able to flow through you.

When does the teacher appear on the scene? When the student is ready. You can't get the teacher to appear if the student isn't ready. The teacher has the power, and the student has the potential. Power needs to be released. It needs to express itself. It needs to reveal itself. However, potential needs to be ready in order for power to be recognized and have its full impact. Two of the key characteristics of readiness are not growing weary and not losing heart, as Paul wrote in Galatians 6:9. The one who has been faithful in the former season demonstrates the character that will sustain him or her in the new season. We will discuss this more extensively in the chapters ahead.

Consider Elijah again. He had no place to release this power. It felt like loneliness. Just think about the language he uses, *"I alone am left"* (1 Kings 19:10). He was in a wilderness, in a cave, and then on a mountain—in every place he seemed lonely and depressed. Why? Your loneliness, your agony comes when you have something to release and nobody is ready to receive it. He was looking for receive-ready ground where the seed of his impartation could find a resting place.

Take the conception process for example. Any creature will tell you there is nothing as laborious as trying to release a seed into a closed womb, a closed mind, an unreceptive audience.

For example, I sow the Word of God as I preach. As much as a pastor, teacher, or preacher would love to help regulate the receptivity of the audience, such is not the case. Instead, the audience largely regulates the flow of the Holy Spirit. No amount of hype and no amount of hoopla can fake a people ready to receive. When they're ready, they are ready. When they are not, they're not. Simple as that. We can press. We can push. We can sow and keep on sowing. Sometimes sheer perseverance starts to break up the ground, and then as one person starts getting hungry, others follow the lead. Generally speaking, though, it is the recipient who controls the flow of the Holy Spirit in his or her life. Power is looking for recipients who are ready. Who are faithful. Who are hungry. Who are pressing in. Who are persevering through.

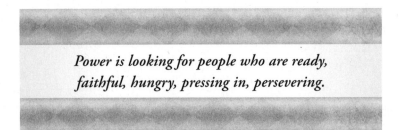

Power is looking for people who are ready, faithful, hungry, pressing in, persevering.

I'm talking beyond preaching. Whatever you offer, wherever you are, and whatever your unique gifting is, for the sake of stewarding it well and not wanting to bang your head against the wall, find ready ground. *Be* the ready ground! Ask the Holy Spirit to bring you into a collision with those who are hungry and receptive—those who will receive and benefit from whatever you carry. It does not matter who you are or what your gift is. If you're a businessperson, the principle is the same. Yes, there is a time for negotiation and salesmanship and marketing; but then there are people and companies that are just not ready to receive what you offer. Recognize this. Identify the relationships that are not ripe for your investment and discern the people who are ready for what you offer. You know what I'm talking about. There are people and situations that are just not ready for the glory that you bring.

On the other side, those who are receive-ready will actually draw the glory out of you. They will pull the revelation, potential, gifting, and anointing right out of you. This is what Elisha did for Elijah. Elisha was receive-ready, and Elijah—the teacher—showed up on the scene. There was a mutual recognition that each man was ready for what the other brought to the table.

There's another person inside you that the world has not seen yet. The time wasn't right before. You had to go through enough trouble, enough pain, enough agony, enough failure to get ready for this moment. But you're ready now. The teacher is appearing. The student is plowing. Remember, you are both the teacher and the student. Continue to sow; but at the same time, understand that to get to your next level, you need to be ready-ground.

Look for a place to make a deposit of everything down inside you while waiting for the deposit that's coming your way. Yes, you're going to talk to some people about it, and they're not going to be to even hear what you have to say. They're not ready for what you're discovering in these pages. Don't be frustrated when someone can't handle your glory, your gifting, you're anointing, your revelation. Don't get upset because the ground is not ready yet. What's the solution? Find someone who has been praying and crying out for what you carry. Make the deposit in his life. Make the deposit in her life. And when the power of what you carry meets the potential inside that person, *something supernatural will happen.*

REFLECTIONS

1. What is the "place of deposit?"

2. Why is it so important for the ground to be receive-ready? How can you be that receive-ready ground?

3. What does the following statement mean to you: "When the student is ready, the teacher will appear?"

CHAPTER 6

IDENTIFYING UNREALIZED POTENTIAL

...Elisha the son of Shaphat, who was plowing
with twelve yoke of oxen before him, and he
was with the twelfth... (1 Kings 19:19).

UNSEEN POTENTIAL

Then Samuel took the horn of oil and anointed him
in the midst of his brothers; and the Spirit of the Lord
came upon David from that day forward... (1 Samuel
16:13).

You carry a glory. There's something deep inside you that requires a meeting with God's power in order to be released. Your potential is awaiting activation. Elisha remains unrealized, unknown, obscure, and unseen until his meeting with Elijah. This is what happened with King David. He was unseen—literally. While his brothers *looked* like royalty, it was the boy with the unseen character and unseen heart of worship and unseen victories over the bear and the lion to whom the prophet Samuel was drawn. He was the man for the mantle. God is looking to bring the unseen into the seen by using power to release your potential.

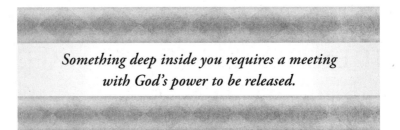

Something deep inside you requires a meeting with God's power to be released.

Scripture is silent about Elisha *until* his meeting with Elijah. We don't get the privilege of learning his backstory. We're not told about his family life. We're left in the dark about his upbringing. Does this mean Elisha was unimportant before Elijah? No. Rather, the Bible gives us a glimpse into select moments where ordinary faithful men and women are launched out into their divine destinies. Before their collisions with power, they are still significant and valuable people. They simply carry unrealized and untapped potential. It's the intersection with power that draws out potential. It's the mantle that brings the unseen into the seen.

Scripture reveals example after example of those who experienced divine intersections with power, saw a release of potential, and ultimately stepped into the momentum of divine purpose.

Noah found favor in God's eyes. He had a family. He had a life. He had a concept of normal. And then God called him to build a boat that would ultimately save the planet. One intersection with power brought Noah out of the unseen into the seen.

Abraham had a story. He had a homeland. *And then God called him out.* Power met Abraham's potential, and he began a journey toward stepping into his purpose. He left his homeland, dwelt in tents as a nomad, and ultimately had a child at an old age through a wife (who was long-passed the age of childbearing) who would go on to establish a heritage for generations to come.

Joseph was unseen until Pharaoh heard that Power enabled him to interpret dreams; he asked Joseph to interpret his own dream and, in turn, made Joseph prime minister of all Egypt.

Moses was an unseen shepherd in the wilderness until Power met him at the burning bush.

David was unseen until Power anointed him and said, *"You're the King of Israel."*

Jesus was even unseen until He was 30 years old and Power opened the heavens and anointed Him.

> *A catalytic collision between God's supernatural power and your potential brings you out of the unseen and into the seen.*

When I say *Power,* I am referring to One Power. I'm not making reference to some ambiguous mysticism. I'm not talking about some otherworldly force or energy. I'm specifically addressing the power of the Most High God. Apart from His power and ability, we can do *nothing* (see John 15:5). In every situation we read about, there is a catalytic collision between God's supernatural power and a person's potential that brings them out of the unseen and into the seen.

Until First Kings 19:19, we do not meet Elisha. He is unseen potential. Elijah hears about him. God gives Elijah instruction on meeting him and what this former plowman will ultimately accomplish. However, until his collision with God's power, Elisha remains out of public view.

Do you feel unseen? Do you feel out of public view? Are you living in that place of obscurity right now? Listen, I realize there are people out there who *want to be seen*. In fact, they *need* to be seen. Their grand pursuit in life is self being seen. They depend on being noticed and recognized and celebrated and catered to in order to maintain their self-worth. That's not what I'm talking about here. You have lived satisfied in the secret place, but you recognize there is something inside you that *you offer* the world. It has not yet been revealed or released. It has nothing to do with you becoming a celebrity or a diva; and has everything to do with you being receive-ready soil.

UNREALIZED POTENTIAL

Do not despise these small beginnings, for the Lord rejoices to see the work begin... (Zechariah 4:10 NLT).

Elisha was not only unseen potential, but he was also unrealized potential. As he plowed, surely he thought to himself, "I don't even know what I've got, but I know that doing what I'm doing is not my destiny." Plowing was a day of small beginnings, but it was the plow that positioned him for the mantle. Elijah found Elisha while he was plowing.

Do you feel like Elisha—that you've got something, maybe you don't even know how to define it, but you know there is something more than what you are currently doing? That ache in the very core of your being, constantly reminding you that where you are cannot define *who* you are and for what you have been created. What you're doing right now cannot shape your vision and expectation of what you will be doing for the rest of your life. We are diligent in our present season, all the while recognizing that the potential inside us is not merely reserved for where we are *right now,* but it's unrealized. In the same way we *realize* that we left our keys on the counter or the same way we *realize* that we left our credit card at the restaurant, there are moments in your life when someone *realizes* the potential inside you. The person recognizes what is there—maybe you don't even see it, but someone does. Power does. When you realize something, it compels you to act. When Elijah realized the potential inside of Elisha, it caused him to pass by and toss his mantle upon him.

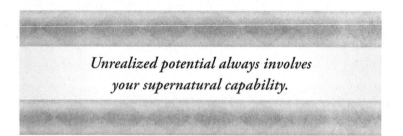

> *Unrealized potential always involves*
> *your supernatural capability.*

Before this incredible transference took place, Elisha had been plowing in the fields. He was working in the dimension of the natural, praying through the pain. Unrealized potential always involves your supernatural capability. The things deep inside you are the very things that solve the deep needs and longings of humanity. This is beyond philanthropy, humanitarianism, and service. While these things are important, they are expressions of what's really inside you. There's supernatural potential burning in your natural frame. While there are gifts, talents, and abilities you have that are clear to everyone who sees you and knows you, Elijah calls out the deeper things. Power calls out the supernatural. Power commissions your ability to accomplish the impossible. Power summons you into the depths. Power invites you into the heights.

Elijah did not walk by Elisha, place his mantle upon him, and invite this plowman into a new dimension of natural work. In other words, Elijah did not summon Elisha into greater levels of plowing. Whether it was plowing in the field of a king, president, or prime minister, the natural act of plowing was not being called out of this man. In the same way, collisions with power, intersections with Elijahs, are not intended to simply upgrade what is already visible in your life. Elijah calls out the deeper things. He summons what's beyond the surface. He calls forth the things we didn't even know we had; and yet we somehow recognize that there is more to life than merely plowing a field.

Don't be satisfied settling for some type of natural upgrade and then calling it supernatural. Supernatural cannot be some term we assign to an extraordinary natural act that we are still capable of accomplishing through our own human effort, ingenuity, and skill. Many of us mistakenly assign the descriptive "supernatural" or "miraculous" to everything that requires just a little bit of extra sweat. I'm not demeaning the things we accomplish as human beings. God divinely knit us together with wisdom, skills, abilities, creative expression, fortitude, grit, gumption, and perseverance to do incredible things. Humankind has built skyscrapers, gone to the moon, painted, sculpted, and created. Because of *how* humans are created, we are capable of creating. We celebrate the potential of humanity. We cheer on what we are capable of doing simply by how we were assembled through divine design. That's not what I want us to focus on right now.

I want to to elevate your thinking little bit. I want to start a riot in your mind when it comes to your true potential. You have the potential to build a building of bricks and mortar, but you also have potential to transform the planet. You have the potential to fly to another galaxy, but also have the potential to change the culture to reflect the Kingdom of God. It might be unrealized right now, but it's there inside you. You have the potential to heal the sick, raise the dead, and set captives free. These realities are possibilities for you, even though they might be unrealized right now.

Unrealized potential causes us to ache to experience the supernatural power that ultimately unveils our true potential to the world.

LOVE THE ACHE AND KEEP PLOWING

Now may the Lord direct your hearts into the love of God and into the patience of Christ (2 Thessalonians 3:5).

I encourage you to love the ache inside that reminds you of what's available, but currently not in operation. Why? Too many of us suppress this ache. We downplay the ache. There's a cry within us for more, but we don't know what to do with it. So many of us try to push mute on this ache for more. It's relentless; but the fact that it is unceasing-until-satisfied should cause us to celebrate what's available rather than settle for what is presently accessible.

Plowing was Elisha's present-accessible reality. However, just because he was faithfully plowing did not mean he was ill-prepared for his moment of power. He was prepared because he did not run off and pursue some counterfeit version of what the deep of him surely longed for. I repeat, there are realities available to you that you are not yet walking in. Don't be disappointed that you are not walking in them...*yet*. Celebrate that they are available to you, and trust the God of Purpose to bring you into greater alignment with your supernatural purpose at His ordained time, through His methods. Remember, purpose is recognized, experienced, and realized through those moments and meetings with power. Patience is absolutely required if we want to protect ourselves from settling for an inferior alternative.

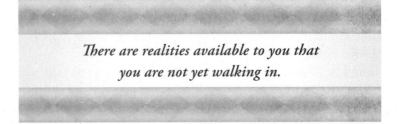

There are realities available to you that you are not yet walking in.

This is what happens to those who are plowing—and grow tired. They become weary. They have not come to love the ache, but rather are desperate to silence its nagging noise. Day after day, night after night as they plow in their place of present assignment, the ache within reminds them that another reality is available. Rather than trusting the God of Purpose and waiting for His power, we give up. We kick the ox. We toss the plow aside. We leave the field—running. Our quest becomes to silence the ache, instead of waiting for God to satisfy it. As a result, we pursue counterfeit solutions to the ache for purpose. Every attempt to satisfy our ache with second-rate pleasures will prolong our true launch into supernatural purpose. We try to access our potential, not through God's power, but through our own pursuits. Our pleasures. Our passions. These things will never ultimately silence the ache within.

Patience prepares us for the power that unleashes our potential. Just as patience protected Elisha from second-rate pursuits and prepared him for Elijah, so our patience actually helps enforce the character and integrity necessary to sustain the power that satisfies the ache. Elisha must be ready in order to receive Elijah's mantle. One key readiness factor is maintaining patience in the process of waiting, while also celebrating the ache that prophesies to us:

"Elijah is coming!"

"Power is at hand!"

"Things you didn't even know you had living inside you are getting ready to come forth!"

I don't believe it was a mistake that Elisha was found plowing, because plowing teaches you how to break up the hard places. Plowing teaches you that you cannot put a good seed in ground that is not prepared. Plowing is a process dedicated to readiness. Plowing teaches you seed time and harvest, sowing and reaping. Plowing teaches you discipline and focus. Plowing teaches you how to follow. Plowing teaches you alignment.

Everything you have ever done has been preparation for what you're about to do.

There's a right kind of people for you to be aligned with, and a wrong kind of people. The ache cries out for the right people and will never be satisfied with the wrong ones. It has to be lined up. Your relationships have to be lined up. You can't go out and plow just anywhere. There's a strategy. There's a structure. There's a purpose. There's a plan. There's a seed. You think you've been doing something that's beneath your anointing, but everything you have ever done has been getting you ready for what you're about to do.

Plowing prepared Elisha for Elijah. Whatever you're doing right now is preparing you for the next level. Everything you have ever done, every job you have ever worked. Everything that you thought was a deadbeat situation, every relationship you thought was beneath you—all of it was training ground for the promotion that is about to break forth in your life. Elijah's coming, and he's looking for a plowing Elisha.

Where will you be found on your day of visitation?

REFLECTIONS

1. What is unseen potential? Unrealized potential?

2. What is "the ache" inside of you? How should you respond to this ache?

3. What are the dangers of impatience while waiting for your moments and meetings with God's power?

PART II

WHEN POWER MEETS POTENTIAL

*...Then Elijah passed by him and threw
his mantle on him* (1 Kings 19:19).

CHAPTER 7

UNWRAP THE GIFT OF EXPOSURE

Then Elijah...threw his mantle on him (1 Kings 19:19).

THE KEY THAT UNLOCKS POTENTIAL

Potential was plowing in the field, all the while waiting for something. Someone. A moment. A miracle. A collision. A release. A deposit. An impartation. An encounter. Potential was waiting for something, not knowing *what* that something would look like. The same is true for you. You carry unseen, unrealized potential. There is an ache inside you, constantly reminding you that *more* is available than you are currently seeing and experiencing. All of the factors are in place. You are following Elisha's example and are faithfully plowing wherever you have been positioned. You are not looking to the right or the left. You're not allowing yourself to become distracted by other pursuits or counterfeit passions. With focus and fortitude you have made a resolution to move forward. You're not quitting. You're not stopping. You're not slowing down. You're not running off. You're not taking an indefinite coffee break. There's something *in* you waiting for something *out* there.

This brings us to the next step in the story of Elijah and Elisha. One day, Elisha looked up and saw Elijah. Potential looked up and saw power. What did power look like? The first expression power took was *exposure*. Exposure is a key that unlocks your potential. Power gives potential exposure. Power can take obscurity, and in a moment, in a second, in an instant—through exposure—bring its potential into full view. Don't ever doubt the life-shaping power of one moment of exposure. You can't buy it. You can't manufacture it. You can't make it happen. Anything you strive after in the realm of exposure will always be a second-rate copy of the exposure released through a divine collision with power.

> *Power can take obscurity and in an instant—through exposure—bring its potential into full view.*

Elisha could have spent his entire life, as many people do, pursuing exposure for himself. Many of us run after something that, once we get it, we only experience its true ability in minor measure. Think about it. Here we are, plowing away, doing what God has called us to do and being where God has called us to be. Again, because of impatience and because we assume we can make something happen more effectively and efficiently than God, we run out and pursue exposure for ourselves.

I'm not saying all forms of pursued exposure are wrong. We need communications divisions. We need marketing campaigns. We need to get our message and materials and products and services out there. But there's a difference between marketing and manipulation. Do you see where I'm coming from? Marketing is stewardship of our services, gifts, talents, abilities, products, and resources, exposing them to people who will benefit from their use—while manipulation is trying to *become someone* through manufacturing exposure.

You can market all day long, that's fine. But when you know that, deep down inside, God has created you for something supernatural and significant, the worst thing you can do is run out and try to manufacture the exposure that will launch you into destiny. Again, exposure through marketing and communications is normal and natural, but the pursuit of exposure to actually fulfill your destiny, become who you were created to be, and step into your purpose is taking matters into your hands that they are not fit to carry.

Remember, only God can set up the exposure that is the key that unlocks your potential and propels you into your purpose.

THE GREAT GIFT THAT POWER DELIVERS

But I have raised you up or this very purpose, that I might show you my power and that my name might be proclaimed in all the earth (Exodus 9:16 NIV).

One moment Elisha was a nobody out plowing fields. In the blink of an eye, he went from being a nobody to becoming successor to the greatest prophet in the land. Surely one of the greatest gifts you can give to anybody is exposure. God did this time after time. Again, reflect on Moses. One moment Moses was an obscure shepherd living in the wilderness; the next he is summoned to deliver a nation and demonstrate the power of God before the world's major superpower, Egypt.

One of the greatest gifts you can receive is exposure. Powerful people have influence, and influence is the foundation of exposure. Influence is what gives substance to exposure. Influence gives someone's exposure worth. Anybody can try to give you exposure. However, the only exposure that has the ability and power to unlock your potential is exposure that comes from a source of value. Again, this source is influence. Only a person with influence has the ability to bring you valuable exposure.

Elijah had something of value to offer Elisha. There are people out there who think they are valuable; but in the end, they are just empty suits. They want influence. They crave power. They pursue recognition. Unfortunately, they are in it for themselves. They are me-centric. You don't want what they have, because they have nothing more than a façade. They might be able to dazzle you for a season, but when the dazzle wears off, they are void of anything raw or real. They are without substance, and its substance that gives value to the exposure you receive.

Wait for the real; don't settle for the phony, the fake, or the flimflam. Impatience compels us to make some ridiculous moves. While waiting and plowing and waiting and plowing, we might see people who appear to "have it all." They look like they've got the power and prestige. You're looking at them, but they are not looking at you. In fact, nothing you do seems to get their attention. This is not God restricting you; this is God preserving you. He is protecting you from falling prey to people who would invariably over-promise and under-deliver. Trust His divine timing. Wait for Elijah. Don't go chasing after every prophet who comes to town. Don't make just anyone your mentor. Don't try to manufacture a meeting with power; when in fact, the person you think offers exposure has nothing to give you.

Elijah was the real deal. He delivered the goods. He had what could push Elisha into the next dimension. The exposure Elijah offered carried significance and weight. He carried true greatness; and when God exposes you to greatness, even for the briefest of moments, if you have potential inside of you, when power passes by that potential, there is a cataclysmic explosion that takes place. Both will always recognize each other. Powerful people recognize potential in people and people of potential know power when they see it. Whenever they pass by one another, potential says, "Now I get it! Now I see it! Now I understand it! Now I realize it!"

Then power says, "Do you know who you are potential? You are standing on the verge. You think you're impressed with this. There's twice as much in you as there is in me, and when we meet…"

Elisha kept plowing and Elijah found him. Depending on what God has called you to do, your moments of exposure *will come*. Not everyone receives the same exposure because not everyone is designed to do the same thing. And remember, exposure comes, not by you chasing after it, but by you remaining faithful in your season, in your moment, in your job, in your family, in your project, in your everyday life. Power that brings exposure is attracted to the faithful, for it is only the faithful who can survive the pressure and weight of exposure.

ARE YOU READY FOR YOUR MOMENT?

Now therefore, fear the Lord, serve Him in sincerity and in truth… (Joshua 24:14).

Faithful plowing reveals a heart that is ripe and ready for an encounter with power. Many people live in the waiting room, not because of God's unwillingness to promote, but because of their unwillingness to be faithful in their current life situation. Faithfulness and integrity are key qualities to promotion through exposure. God is seeking those who serve Him in *sincerity and truth*. He's looking for those who are hungry for the next level, but also understand that the key to stepping into that level is being faithful where they are.

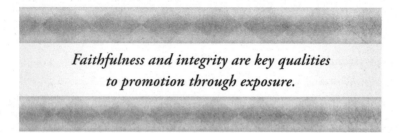

> **Faithfulness and integrity are key qualities to promotion through exposure.**

Exposure is the greatest of blessings for the one who carries potential and stewards it well through a lifestyle of steadfastness, faithfulness, and integrity. This person is poised for the touch of power that releases the exposure needed for living in the next dimension. However, exposure can bring complete destruction and untold ruin to the life that is not ready for everything that accompanies it. God denies exposure for the sake of protection, not restriction. Anything that would hinder us from walking into our purpose is a red flag as far as Heaven is concerned.

Many have been crushed by pre-season promotion. They have pushed their way through the crowd, and instead of waiting for divine timing, they knocked down the door and did what they could in order to secure the object of their desire. A promotion, a blessing, or a breakthrough received before we are ready for it can crush us under its weight. This is not to say God expects perfection from those He blesses. Time after time, it's His blessings that invite us into new levels of maturity and development. At the same time, I am not referring to a deliverance from bondage or healing from a disease right now. I am talking about a promotion that takes you into a new level, a new dimension, and a new season of life.

If you don't have what it takes to stand strong in your new season, then the very thing that was meant for your blessing, could harm or even destroy you pre-season. This is why patience cannot be emphasized enough. Elisha did not find Elijah pre-season. That mantle could have killed him before that divine moment. The responsibility would have been too much for him. He needed to plow more. He needed to learn the value of hard work, time management, and discipline. Elisha was not perfect when Elijah found him, but he was prepared. He was ready for his moment.

Are you ready for yours?

I assure you, as you continue to faithfully plow in this season, God Almighty is faithfully preparing you for the next. Every moment you continue in the natural, faithfully plowing, faithfully working, faithfully going to school, faithfully serving, something supernatural is taking place behind the veil. Your lifestyle of faithfulness attracts the gaze of Heaven. Every moment you stick to the plowing process, you are becoming more and more fit for your meeting of power and moment of exposure.

You don't even know what's going on inside you. You are gloriously clueless to what the Creator is working on and weaving behind the scenes. You may feel like you're sitting in the back. You might feel unnoticed and unrecognized. You may even feel like saying, "If I have to plow one more day, one more time, one more moment, I'm gonna throw that thing in the ditch." Yet there is something pushing you. Someone is compelling you to keep going. Keep plowing. Keep reading. Keep studying. Keep working. Keep giving. It doesn't matter if no one knows your name. You may have no recognition whatsoever.

The truth is, you are potential ready for action. There's potential energy inside you just waiting for that push of kinetic power. You are stationary until that one bump, one push, or one spark comes along and launches you right into the next dimension.

Your moment is at hand. That's why you can't be satisfied. That's why you can't sit back and look around. You are potential waiting for power to release you into your moment. You're just waiting for the hookup. And as soon as you get that hookup, you're going to go up. You're next in line for the hookup. You are not forgotten. You are not on some shelf somewhere. The eyes of the Lord God are upon you. His favor surrounds you. His glory is within you. His power is around you.

You've been plowing in the field waiting for the right time, waiting to be in the right place, and waiting for the right mantle to pass over you. Get ready. Power is coming that will expose your potential and unlock your purpose.

REFLECTIONS

1. How is exposure valuable when it comes to releasing your potential?

2. Is it possible to pursue false exposure?

3. What happens if you experience exposure before you are ready for your moment? Why would God deny exposure to you?

CHAPTER 8

RECOGNIZE YOUR MOMENT

*And he left the oxen and ran after Elijah, and
said, "Please let me kiss my father and my mother,
and then I will follow you..." (1 Kings 19:20).*

ARE YOU READY?

*No one, having put his hand to the plow, and looking
back, is fit for the kingdom of God (Luke 9:62).*

When Elijah shows up, everything changes. When our moment
comes, we must be ready. Elisha recognized his moment. He was
ready. This is why God denies moments of power to those *before*
their moment is ready. We just saw how a moment that transitions you from one season to the next can actually be deadly if
you are ill-prepared for the moment.

I want to help you get ready, so that when Elijah shows up,
you can recognize the arrival of the moment that changes everything. Because let me tell you, when that moment comes, you
can't go back to who you were. You won't be able to. *When you
catch a glimpse of what you have been called into, what you're being
called out of will never satisfy you again.* To return to what you
are being called out of would be living beneath what has become

available. I believe God does everything in His power to make this type of regression impossible. Does it happen? Sadly, yes. But not to you. Don't let it happen to you. Be the one who embraces the journey. Go from glory to glory and strength to strength.

Look at Elisha's moment:

> *Elisha left the oxen standing there, ran after Elijah, and said to him, "First let me go and kiss my father and mother good-bye, and then I will go with you!" Elijah replied, "Go on back, but think about what I have done to you"* (1 Kings 19:20 NLT).

Elisha was ready for his moment, absolutely. When he tells Elijah that he is going to back and kiss his father and mother good-bye, he is not behaving like the example Jesus gives us in Luke 9:61, who says,

> *"Lord, I will follow You, but let me first go and bid them farewell who are at my house."*

There are two different perspectives here. Let's contrast these two accounts. Elisha was ready for his next season, but still returned to his household, while the people in Luke's Gospel account are obviously *not* ready for their next season.

No Turning Back

In Luke 9, Jesus gives examples of those who would be crushed by the weight of discipleship if they had continued on with Him while maintaining the attitudes and paradigms they demonstrated. Read what happened:

> *Now it happened as they journeyed on the road, that someone said to Him, "Lord, I will follow You wherever*

You go." And Jesus said to him, "Foxes have holes and birds of the air have nests, but the Son of Man has nowhere to lay His head." Then He said to another, "Follow Me." But he said, "Lord, let me first go and bury my father." Jesus said to him, "Let the dead bury their own dead, but you go and preach the kingdom of God." And another also said, "Lord, I will follow You, but let me first go and bid them farewell who are at my house." But Jesus said to him, "No one, having put his hand to the plow, and looking back, is fit for the kingdom of God" (Luke 9:57-62).

Even though the situations each of the people in Luke 9 discussed seemed valid—from the one who wanted to bury his father to the one who wanted to bid farewell to his household—context is what assigns meaning to what was taking place in this text. It was not a parable. It was not a story. It was reality. Jesus was journeying on the road, and came across at least three different people who wanted to follow Him, but also wanted to go their own way. They wanted a mixture. It had little to do with just burying a father or saying good-bye to family members. Hearts were divided. They did not recognize the power that was passing them by, power that could unlock their potential and push them into their next seasons. Jesus had this power; sadly, the three examples we read about were ill-prepared for their moments of visitation.

Even though Jesus was asking them to make some significant sacrifices at the same time, He was inviting them to journey along the same road He was traveling. There is no greater fulfillment to the question, *What's my purpose in life?* than to be one who journeys alongside Jesus.

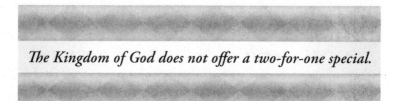

The Kingdom of God does not offer a two-for-one special.

The three individuals in Luke 9 wanted both Jesus *and* their way. The Kingdom of God does not offer a two-for-one special, where we get the best of God and the best of mediocrity. The best of the Kingdom and the best of the world. The best of the holy and the best of the vile. The best of the glory and the best of the profane. In fact, there is no room for God's best and second rate to take up residence together. They will not peacefully cohabitate. One will rule the day. Our hearts don't have the capacity for dual-surrendering. We either yield to God, or we turn back and go our own way. Jesus recognized this, and knew that these individuals did not recognize their moment. If they truly knew who was standing before them, inviting them into a lifestyle of journeying the same road as He, the attachments that they ended up listing would have been non-issues. Why? Because when potential recognizes its moment of power, it responds appropriately. This reveals the maturity of the one carrying potential.

Excuses reveal immaturity. Remember, immaturity demonstrates that we will not hold up under the weight and pressure of promotion. Perfection is not required for promotion, but there is a degree of maturity that is required in order to sustain us during the period of transition into a new season. Jesus gives us three examples of immature people who had potential, but were not ready for their intersection with power.

WHAT'S ON THE OTHER SIDE?

Think about it. These three people in Luke 9 *could* have been disciples. They could have joined the ranks of those who turned the world upside down (see Acts 17:6). Their hands could have been used to heal the sick, diseased, leprous, and maligned. They could have been mouthpieces touched by the fiery words of Heaven to preach the piercing and powerful truth of the gospel. They could have trampled upon all the works of the enemy (see Luke 10:19). They *could* have released their potential and gone down in history as those who were *"with Jesus"* (see Acts 4:13).

We have just reviewed what these people *could* have done with their potential. So what happened? They did not recognize their moment standing right before them. They did not have a vision for what was on the other side of Jesus' invitation.

A divided heart delivers the wrong answer when power walks up and invites you to join Him on the journey.

I encourage you, be ready for your moment. There's nothing for you back there. You know where "back there" is. I'm not telling you to leave your family. I'm not asking you to go overseas. I'm not saying sell the dog, trade in the car for a jalopy, and completely rearrange your current living situation. Jesus was more focused on their hearts than He was their externals. Family is not bad. Attending funerals is not wrong. Rather, it's a divided heart that delivers the wrong answer when power walks up and invites you to join Him on the journey.

Be sure that your heart is undivided when power reveals itself. So many of us want the perks of power without the anchor of responsibility. This is not possible. For power to be released, and ultimately sustained, it requires a suitable resting place. In order for your potential to be released, you must be a willing and obedient vessel that power can touch and make demands of. Power knows better. Power is touching you because it knows where it can take you. However, power requires your cooperation. It will not drag you kicking and screaming, spitting and clawing. Power is looking for those who say will say "Yes" to its invitation.

What could have happened to these would-be disciples along the road if they responded to their moment? I believe Luke gives us a glimpse of what would have been possible for those who said "No" to Jesus because they wanted their next season on their own terms. The concluding verses of Luke 9 transition seamlessly into Luke 10, where we are given a vision of what would have been available to the disciples who settled for second rate when power was beckoning them.

Let's briefly look through Luke 10:1-9:

> *After these things the Lord appointed seventy others also, and sent them two by two before His face into every city and place where He Himself was about to go* (Luke 10:1).

After *what* things? Jesus identified those ready for their moment and positioned for their next season. It's amazing how quickly this season was coming. Think about it. Those who said "No" to Jesus' invitation said "No" to a whole new way of living that was just around the corner.

Those who recognized the cost and responded to their moment were commissioned as the "seventy others" who become sent ones. To become a "sent one," we must respond appropriately to the moment standing before us. Power stood before these disciples, ready and eager to call out their potential. Power would not have even approached these individuals if there was no potential. In the same way, power wants to visit you. Power wants to unleash what's inside you and turn someone who was walking along the road of life into a royal ambassador sent to announce the advancing Kingdom of God. Power takes ordinary plowmen and turns them into anointed prophets.

We read on:

> Then He said to them, "The harvest truly is great, but the laborers are few; therefore pray the Lord of the harvest to send out laborers into His harvest. Go your way; behold, I send you out as lambs among wolves. Carry neither money bag, knapsack, nor sandals; and greet no one along the road. But whatever house you enter, first say, 'Peace to this house.' And if a son of peace is there, your peace will rest on it; if not, it will return to you. And remain in the same house, eating and drinking such things as they give, for the laborer is worthy of his wages. Do not go from house to house. Whatever city you enter, and they receive you, eat such things as are set before you. And heal the sick there, and say to them, 'The kingdom of God has come near to you'" (Luke 10:1-9).

This was the lifestyle that Jesus was summoning people into; and ultimately this is what they were saying no to. Jesus was calling forth laborers who would heal the sick, raise the dead, and destroy the works of the devil. He was commissioning disciples to step into their purpose as spokespeople for an eternal, unshakeable Kingdom.

Your response to power's invitation has enormous implications. If those walking along the road would have said yes to Jesus, they would have been immediately launched into the Luke 10 lifestyle we just read about. Unfortunately, their moment walked right up to them and they were not ready.

Are you ready? I want you to be. That is why we are going through these stories. This is why we are looking at these examples. I want to overwhelm you with information and truth and revelation that positions you to be on the ready line when your moment of power arrives.

ELISHA'S RESPONSE

On the other end, we notice Elisha's response to Elijah. At first glance, how Elisha reacts does not seem all that different from the would-be disciples of Luke 9. Look again, because it's all about context. The difference between Elisha and the disciples who never made the cut was that the plowman was ready. It's ultimately not about saying good-bye to your family or friends. It's not about giving a funeral or having a wedding. It's not about whether you go back to your town and throw a party and pass around meat to all the townspeople. It's about being ready for your moment when power meets potential.

Power hit potential when Elijah tossed his mantle upon Elisha. The man got hit, and he could not go back to normal. Something inside him changed. Even though he went back to kiss mom and dad good-bye, an allegiance had been broken inside him. In Luke 9, the soul ties were still there. Those people were unwilling to follow Jesus and respond to His invitation because their hearts were knit to something, someone, or some life. Elisha got hit with a mantle and was messed up. He was ruined for old ways and the old days. Even though the text tells us that he went back, his heart never went back. In fact, going back was Elisha's test. We'll look at this in more detail toward the end of our time together, but God has different tests for different people. They are custom-made, for He evaluates us on an individual level.

I think that as Elisha prepared the farewell feast for his townsfolk, people were asking him, "Elisha, what are you doing? Where are you going? Why are you going off with that prophet? Why are you throwing your life away? Why don't you settle down? Get married. Have some kids. Get a good job. Work on your portfolio. Build up your retirement. Go on vacation. Carry on the family business."

Something kept Elisha's heart ready and receptive for transition. It was Elijah's response. After Elisha told his new mentor that he planned on going back home to say good-bye and throw a party, Elijah did not deem it a deal breaker. Elijah did not call him unfit for the new dimension he was being called into. It was obvious that Elisha was ready for his moment. All Elijah said was, *"Go on back, but think about what I have done to you"* (1 Kings 19:20b NLT). That's all Elijah *needed* to say.

When Elisha went home in the natural, his heart was still with Elijah. His allegiance was still with his invitation into the next season, new dimension, and greater glory. He was ruined and wrecked. I have to believe that during his trip back home, after crossing paths with Elijah, the former plowman was thinking:

> I can't go back to being who I was. I can't act like it didn't happen. I can't ignore this whole new level of glory. I can't sit in that same place, even though loving

hands pushed me there. I can't stay there, Mama. I love you, Daddy, it's been real. I know you had a plan for my future, and I hate to mess that up, but I've been exposed to power on another level, and I've got to go into the next dimension.

> *One collision with power and you will*
> *never go back to normal again.*

Get ready to step into your next dimension, into your next flame of glory, into your next supernatural release, into your next realm of the power of God. Like Elisha, you're being set up for an encounter with the glory of God. You're on track to getting all messed up. One collision with power and you will never be able to go back to normal again. There's no normal anymore. Normal has been redefined, upgraded, and supercharged. Your normal is now a whole new level!

REFLECTIONS

1. In Luke 9:57-62, what prevented the three people from recognizing their moment and responding to Jesus?

2. What's on the other side of correctly re sponding to your moment?

3. How was Elisha's response to Elijah different from the examples in Luke 9?

CHAPTER 9

RESPOND TO YOUR MOMENT

Then he [Elisha] arose and followed
Elijah... (1 Kings 19:21).

RUINED FOR THE OLD LEVEL

Do not remember the former things, nor consider the
things of old. Behold, I will do a new thing, now it
shall spring forth; shall you not know it? I will even
make a road in the wilderness and rivers in the desert
(Isaiah 43:17-19).

Elisha had a meeting with power that redefined and reoriented his entire life. That's what power does to potential. When potential is ready for its intersection with power, and the two collide, there is no going back. There is only one travel option—forward. Onward. Upward. The first thing we see is that Elisha *"arose and followed Elijah"* (1 Kings 19:21). It's time for you to arise and respond to your meeting with power.

In the previous chapter, we saw how Elisha's collision with power rendered him utterly useless in his old season. When your potential is called out by one moment with power, you become wrecked for living in your former season. You arise. You lift up your eyes. You see things on a new dimension. You see what you had not seen before. When you're ready for that new season and your moment comes, and power touches your life and releases what's inside you, there is no going back. You can try, but your plan will be foiled.

Someone may call and want you to come back, but the level of anointing that's been released over your life cries out, "No, I won't settle for the old times, the old ways, the old fun, the old games, the old talk, the old hangouts. That satisfied me in my old season. That met some need inside of me while living in my former level. But you don't understand, I've been touched by power. Power was waiting all along. While we were having fun, the Maker of Heaven and earth was arranging a meeting. When we were hanging out, God Almighty was orchestrating a divine setup. He was getting ready for my new glory. When we were on the golf course, in the hair salon, having a cheeseburger, something was happening in the unseen realm. You didn't see it, and I didn't know it, but something inside me was getting restless. Power was getting ready to come on the scene and show me who I was and what was inside me. Now, I just can't go back!" Surely thoughts of this kind consumed Elisha's mind as he walked through town and around his old neighborhood.

Elijah recognized that the touch of power would utterly ruin Elisha for everything that was back home, in his old version of normal. We read that on Elisha's trip to say good-bye to his old season, his old life, his old ways, his old routines, his old normals, his old friends, and his old job, he must have taken Elijah's instruction to heart. When Elisha asked permission to go back home, Elijah did not scold or condemn him; he just left him with something to ponder. Elijah said, *"Go on back, but think about what I have done to you"* (1 Kings 19:20 NLT). I have to think that this one thought kept him ruined for the old while still interacting with the old.

This is not some call to isolate yourself like a hermit. There are people and places that will not change, even when you are touched. Those collisions with power call out *your* potential; they do not call it out for others. Each person must experience his or her own moment where power touches that person's potential. It's an intimate experience. Elijah's mantle was ready for Elisha—no one else. Even though there were 7,000 who had not bowed their knees to Baal and played the harlot before false gods, Elisha was the man who got the mantle.

As you come into contact with certain elements of your old level, don't belittle them. Don't shame them. Don't elevate yourself into some "above the rest," superiority position. God ordained you to make a transition from the old to the new for His purpose at this season according to His will. If others aren't there, just remember what took place in your life. If they try to invite you into their ways and activities, which were *your* old ways and old activities, smile and decline. You don't need to condemn others for not making the transition yet, just as others did not condemn you in your previous level. God is patient with His people. He has a plan. Some just cooperate with it easier or more quickly than others. Rather than making anyone feel poorly about where they are, simply *live* at your new level. Speak at your new level. Operate at your new level. Don't flaunt it around. It's normal. It's natural. It's seamless. It feels right. It sounds good. This is just how you live now.

Normal for you is the next level for somebody else. Live at your new normal, keeping in mind that your lifestyle is calling other people up higher. They see your potential released and something starts stirring within them. They see you operating in your gifts and talents, and they start wanting to steward what they have been given. Just encourage them to be faithful. That was the key factor that positioned you for the mantle transference.

Remember, Elisha faithfully plowed. He didn't run around looking for his moment. He didn't go to every service, conference, crusade, seminar, and motivational talk seeking out his moment. He was faithful in his old season and this positioned him to respond correctly at the most significant transition of his life. Most likely, Elisha had to deal with some of this thinking when he went back home to say good-bye to his old level. There was a whole town of people who were living in Elisha's old level.

Maybe there is a whole workplace of people living at your old level. Maybe you're in a house filled with people living at your old level. Maybe you are roommates with someone living on your old level. The best way you can summon them upward is by living at your new level as *normal*. It's no longer your next dimension—it's your normal dimension. It was the next level when you were living at the old level. It was an upgrade when you were out in the field, plowing. But that was no longer the case for Elisha. The mantle was placed upon him. The next level quickly became his new level. The same is true for you!

HOW TO BE LAUNCHED BY A MOMENT

The Lord was with Joseph, and he became a successful man, and he was in the house of his Egyptian master. His master saw that the Lord was with him and that the Lord caused all that he did to succeed in his hands. So Joseph found favor in his sight and attended him, and he made him overseer of his house and put him in charge of all that he had (Genesis 39:2-4 ESV).

Now I want us to look at what it means to live in this new dimension we have been launched into. There are people who get launched, but never learn how to live. They experience success, but they don't become *successful* like Joseph. They don't embrace a perspective where the touch of power transforms their entire mode of living. There are people who do experience a legitimate touch of power. It shakes them. It rattles them. It shifts stuff around. It heals. It delivers. It releases. It gives freedom. It makes them feel all good inside. Quickly, they were exposed to another dimension. The invitation was issued.

Now it's time to learn how to function at this new capacity. An experience is great, but it must be the gateway into something. It's one thing to stick your finger into an electrical socket and get shocked, but it's something else to learn how to live with a finger stuck in that socket. That's what I'm calling you to do. No, you're not always going to feel some zing, but you're going to recognize that what you felt, sensed, and experienced launched you into a new dimension of living. Going back is not an option. I want you to have eyes that not only recognize your moment, but learn how to move forward *after* the moment.

Look at Elijah. All he did was pass Elisha by and let his mantle pass over the plowman. This was the moment when true power was exposed to true potential. Something happened in that moment that was undeniable and crystal clear. In fact, it was as if potential responded before power did. Power passed by potential, but potential dropped everything and ran after power. Again, potential recognized its moment. Potential quickly responded when power passed on by. Read it again, *"Then Elijah passed by him and threw his mantle on him. And he left the oxen and ran after Elijah"* (1 Kings 19:19-20). Elijah was ready for the next dimension. Not only did he recognize power's arrival, but he responded. He ran after it. You've got to want it that much.

God sovereignly sets you up, but you have to want it. You have to respond. You have to choose it. You have to run after it. When He brings you into a moment of power, don't fall down, spin around, jump on your head, and think to yourself, *Wow, that was a powerful touch!* The touch is never designed just to touch—the touch of power is designed to release you into the new level. Your moment is not about a moment, it's about a dramatic collision that will set the course of a whole new trajectory for your life.

Too many receive the touch, but don't follow the Teacher. Therein lies the test. Those who will not steward their moment are ultimately unable to step into a new season at that particular time of life. It doesn't mean God is done with them. It doesn't mean Jesus has passed them by. It just means there is more plowing to do. It just means that maturity, integrity, steadfastness, honor, and character need to be developed before people start living and functioning at a new dimension as a new normal.

You see, many are content to set up camp on the outskirts of a new dimension. They are fine fishing in the shallows when His voice beckons them into the deep. They camp out on their moments of power, believing that the moment was all there was. Your moment was never designed to be sufficient—it was purposed to be a launching pad. Consider how a diving board is not the final end, the pool is. People can jump up and down on a diving board all they want, it does not mean they are going to be launched from one level to the next, from land to water, from air to pool. Too many people live their lives jumping up and down on the diving board. Some moments might take them very high where they have dramatic encounters with power. Just because you jump up does not mean you jump forward. Just because you go up does not mean you go out. I've been assigned to call you up and send you out.

This "up and down" thought process reveals that the person is not yet fit to go beyond the moment, jump forward, and step into the lifestyle. Imagine if Elisha had responded the way so many people today do to their moments of power. If you can, try to re-imagine the account in First Kings 19. Elisha could have been plowing, caught the mantle, fell down, rolled around, did some back flips, and then gone right back to plowing the same way he had always done it. He could have kept on jumping up and down on the diving board—his moment with Elijah just adding some spring to his step.

Let's never reduce encounters with power to something that adds spring to our step. This is laughable. God does not bring Heaven's electricity into your life to simply give you a thrill, but rather to give you a glimpse of what a new dimension of living looks like. The shock of the collision wakes you up to new levels of glory, anointing, power, realized potential, and activated purpose.

RESPOND TO YOUR MOMENT

The key is response. We must respond to our moment in order to live at another level. In order for potential to become released, we must respond to our moment of power. In the previous chapter, we discovered how important it is to recognize your moment of power when it's standing before you. Elisha recognized Elijah and ran after him. Even after going back home and tying up some loose ends, Elisha still *arose* and followed him.

On the other side, the three people mentioned in Luke 9 did not realize the power of their moment, for they all responded poorly to their meetings with Jesus. They encountered Him, but they did not follow Him. They had a moment, but the moment did not change or transform them. They were still clinging on to the comfort and safety of their former level of living. That's what they knew. That's what made sense. That's what they understood. The new level of living Jesus was extending their way was unsafe. It was radical. It was upside down. It was supernatural. They met Power as He walked down the road, but ultimately, they did not allow their moment with Power to launch them into a new dimension. That new dimension would have likely meant their inclusion among the disciples in Luke 10 who were commissioned to transform the landscape of the known world. They were sent out as laborers, purposed to preach a new Kingdom and release the power of God. Truly, the 70 people in Luke 10 responded correctly to their moment of visitation, while the three nameless individuals in Luke 9 did not.

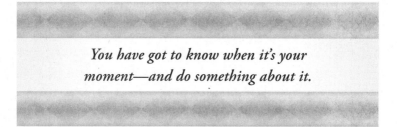

You have got to know when it's your moment—and do something about it.

You have got to know when it's your moment—and do something about it. You've got to want it. Blind Bartimaeus knew when it was his moment, and even though they told him to shut up, shut up, *shut up,* he said, "I can't shut up! This is *my* moment!" The man had an obvious impediment—his blindness. This could have been his excuse to bypass his moment. This could have been his easy out. This could have been his license to wallow in his old level and continue to be defined as *Blind Bartimaeus.* He decided to take another route. He used every faculty available to step into another level. Even though he could not see, he used what he had available—his hearing—to respond to his moment. In Mark 10:47 we read how the story unfolds, *"And when he heard that it was Jesus of Nazareth, he began to cry out and say, 'Jesus, Son of David, have mercy on me!'"* He responded to his moment.

Even though Bartimaeus had a physical handicap and although he experienced some significant resistance, he still used what he had to step into this moment. Why? He recognized what was on the other side of his collision with power. People told him to shut up, but he took that as fuel to cry out all the more and all the louder.

What are people telling you? Are they trying to keep you from stepping into your new season? Are they wanting to restrain you from launching into a new dimension, only to maintain you at their level? Press through. Recognize your moment and run after it like Elisha did. Silence the crowd by crying out louder like Bartimaeus did. Press through the crowd like the woman with the issue of blood (see Mark 5:25-34). They saw their moments and responded. They were not content to let power pass them by. They weren't after a fleeting touch or a mere experience. They recognized that the touch of power was simply a transfer point that would launch them from one dimension to the next. From plowman to prophet. From blind man to disciple who could see (see Mark 10:52). From woman with a non-stop flow of blood to a daughter of God, healed and whole (see Mark 5:34). On the other side of each collision of power was a transformed life that still speaks to us today.

REFLECTIONS

1. What does it mean to be "ruined for your old level of living?" What does this look like for you?

2. Is it possible to experience a touch of power but not see your life changed? What would this look like?

3. Can you identify examples of people who correctly responded to their moments of power and stepped into a new level?

CHAPTER 10

SEIZE YOUR MOMENT

...and [Elisha] became his [Elijah's]
servant (1 Kings 19:21).

THE VALUE OF YOUR MOMENT

Elisha did not just receive a touch of power—he allowed that touch to transform his very identity. In First Kings 19:21, we see the result of Elisha's encounter with Elijah. He allowed the touch to transform him from plowman to Elijah's *servant*. This is why your meeting with power is so vital and valuable. The key was *how* Elisha responded to the moment. He was not casual or cool about it. He was not lazy. He was not idle. Rather, he *seized* the moment and allowed it to transform him. We seize what we recognize as valuable and transformative.

> *You seize what you recognize as*
> *valuable and transformative.*

A moment of power is never given simply for the purpose of thrills and emotionalism. It is a transfer point. Don't be content to simply camp out on the outskirts, when your moment has the power to call something out of you that *only* functions at a new, higher level. This is why stuff inside of you has not come to the surface yet. It's not that you don't have what it takes; you do. However, what's inside you is prepared and positioned for another level. If it came forth now, it would be destructive. If you started imparting and offering and sharing and releasing what you currently have stored up inside, no one would get it. You'd be written off. They'd call you crazy. You've gone off the deep end.

I understand that with the release of potential, levels of persecution and resistance do come. However, there is also resistance that comes when we try to step out into our next season too early. What's inside of you requires an intersection with power. The meeting is divine. It is sovereignly staged. But remember, God does not set up these meetings just so you can get some type of spiritual high off the flowing current of His power. Your moment is intentional. It's designed to launch you into a new level where everything inside you will have its place to come forth.

Bartimaeus needed the divine intersection with the power of Jesus in order to become who he was created to be—a healed, seeing follower of the Lamb of God. He could not have made that happen in his own strength, nor could he have received any benefit from just seeking a touch without transformation. Every touch is designed for transformation. In Mark 5, the woman with the constant flow of blood reached out and touched the hem of Jesus' garment. Power proceeded out of Him and ushered that woman into a transformative moment where her identity shifted. No longer was she the woman with the *"issue of blood"* (see Mark 5:25 KJV). Her moment changed her into one Jesus called *"Daughter,"* whose response to that moment *"made thee whole"* (see Mark 5:34 KJV).

Both these individuals pressed their way into transformation. They recognized the immeasurable value of a moment. Don't be content to simply receive a touch, when in fact God desires to release transformation. Bartimaeus would not have risked greater ridicule and cried out among the crowd if he did not expect a touch that transformed. In the same way, the woman with the constant blood flow would not have left her home, crawled out into a very public place—where crowds were gathered around Jesus—and pushed herself through the people to simply touch the edge of his robe if there was no expectation of transformation attached to this touch. She was not looking to feel good; she was looking to receive wholeness. She didn't want to live in her current level with some bells and whistles added; she wanted to step into a whole new dimension of living. The value of these moment compelled each person to press through to Jesus.

Bartimaeus would not shut up. The woman didn't care if she had to crawl through the dirt in order to touch Power. This must be our attitude when stepping into our new level. We should have no other approach to the transformative touch of power. I can't repeat it enough. A zing won't change you. Running around the building won't escort you to another level. You can touch the fire, feel the wind, and taste the rain, but if the extraordinary feelings that a touch of power brings are not accompanied by an extraordinary transformation, you're simply staying where you are with a good memory of how, one day, Elijah threw something on you and it made you feel good— but you didn't do anything with it. You'll daydream about the exciting moment when Jesus came through town, and you didn't run, push, crawl, wiggle, bicycle, or skateboard to get through the crowds and receive the touch that transformed everything. Why didn't you push through and receive from Him? You will never benefit from a moment of power if you do not recognize its value *beyond* a temporary feeling. You won't risk everything for a temporary feeling, but you will for a transformation.

VISION PRODUCES RESOLVE AND TENACITY INSIDE YOU

Where there is no prophetic vision the people cast off restraint... (Proverbs 29:18 ESV).

Your moment is valuable because it has the ability to draw out your potential, and in turn completely transform your identity. This is exactly what happened with Elisha. He responded correctly to his touch of power by following Elijah; and as a result of properly handling his moment, he went from plowman to prophet. The same is true for you. When you have a vision for what your moment has the ability to produce in your life, you become tenacious. You have relentless resolve. You're not only going to get touched by a moment, but you are going to step into your moment.

People often experience a moment without ever stepping into the potential of that moment. This is what gets you from one level to the next. When you begin to visualize the other side of your moment, you become like the people in the Gospel accounts who cast all inhibition aside because they knew their moment with Jesus would change everything. They seized it at all costs.

Is this you?

When your moment comes, don't just stand around. Start running. Your moment of power is an invitation into a lifestyle of unleashed potential and realized purpose. That's beyond valuable! People spend all their lives chasing after these things. The wealthiest individuals on the planet would gladly surrender their entire fortune for the very thing that presents itself to you in the form of a moment. Why? That moment unlocks the door to a greater release of your potential and greater fulfillment of your purpose.

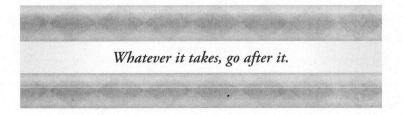

Whatever it takes, go after it.

Whatever it takes, go after it. If you have to crawl, resolve to crawl into your moment. If you're knocked down on your knees, it doesn't matter. You're still coming in. This is tenacity. This is resolve. This is the grit that demonstrates whether or not you value what your moment has unlocked. Greater levels of living are not for the faint of heart. God protects people from greater levels if they don't see the value, and in turn don't exhibit the vigor to walk upon these high places.

Think about the exchange between Elijah and Elisha. Elijah, the teacher, doesn't even realize the magnitude of what took place by exposing potential to power. He kept on walking. Was he ignorant? No. At the same time, he was waiting to see what would happen. Did Elisha, the student, value the touch? How was this plowman going to steward the mantle that was tossed upon him? Was he going to celebrate the touch and go back to plowing, or was the plowman going to receive the invitation to become a prophet.

Think about what happened between Jesus and the woman with the flow of blood. Many people were touching Him, but there was a touch that produced transformation. In fact, when the afflicted woman touched Jesus, Scripture tells us that *"power had gone out of Him"* (see Mark 5:30). Jesus turned around and asked, *"Who touched My clothes?"* The disciples surely thought to themselves, "What is He hollering about?" They explained to Jesus, *"You see the multitude thronging You, and You say, 'Who touched Me?'"* (Mark 5:31). But there was something special about this woman's touch. Scripture does not give us any additional clarity as to whether or not all of the other people who were thronging and touching Jesus were actually receiving from Him. Maybe they were, maybe not. Vision is what caused this audacious woman to step into her moment. She had a vision for what touching Jesus would produce in her life.

Even on her way to meet the Miracle Man, she was filled with vision and expectation. We read that *"she said, 'If only I may touch His clothes, I shall be made well'"* (Mark 5:28). In the Amplified Bible we are given a greater glimpse of how this woman responded to this vision. We read that *"she kept saying, 'If I only touch His garments, I shall be restored to health.'"* This was not some type of mantra. This was not a positive confession. This was not "put your mind to it, envision the outcome, and poof—it just happens out of the blue." This woman was driven by a very clear vision. She knew the touch of His power would unlock her potential. Her potential was wholeness. Her potential was receiving healing. Her potential was living without the incessant flow of blood that plagued her for twelve long, hard years. She had a vision for how the touch of power would unlock and release her potential so that, ultimately, she could fulfill her purpose. Power unleashes potential—and potential enables us to do what we have been designed to do.

This woman was restricted by her affliction. Her obstacle held her back from stepping into new levels of living and ultimately, hindered her from fulfilling her purpose. Power destroys restrictions. It breaks through the chains that have held our potential hostage. The key is recognizing and responding to power when it shows up on the scene. When it walks in the door, something inside you will start leaping. What's happening? The potential inside you recognizes that the power that just walked in is the power that will draw potential out.

DON'T LET YOUR TRANSITION PASS YOU BY

He who has a slack hand becomes poor, but the hand of the diligent makes rich (Proverbs 10:4).

Don't have a "slack hand" when it comes to seizing your moment. Proverbs 10:4 is a key for putting this principle into proper use. You have to grab it when it comes, and you have to hold on to it. If you don't seize it, you become poor. I'm not just talking about money. There are people with more money than they know what to do with, but they are still poor because they refuse to seize their moment.

Let's go back to Blind Bartimaeus. While the woman with the issue of blood took hold of her moment, Bartimaeus refused to let his moment pass him by. He knew that the power Jesus carried would unleash his potential and transition him to a new level. Jesus was passing through town, and this man responded. Let's look at the context and note the similarity between Bartimaeus and Elisha.

> *Now they came to Jericho. As He [Jesus] went out of Jericho with His disciples and a great multitude, blind Bartimaeus, the son of Timaeus, sat by the road begging. And when he heard that it was Jesus of Nazareth, he began to cry out and say, "Jesus, Son of David, have mercy on me!"* (Mark 10:46-47)

Just as Elisha could have missed Elijah, so Bartimaeus could have missed his moment with Jesus. Bartimaeus responded to the fact that Jesus was coming through town. He started to cry out. People tried to shut him up, but this became fuel for the fire. He upgraded his cry. He got louder. Maybe he got a bit wilder. He did whatever he could to get noticed—and he was. We see that *"Jesus stood still and commanded him to be called"* (Mark 10:49). This was Bartimaeus' moment. And yet, it seemed like there was the possibility that he could have missed it—even now. Follow the rest of his story:

> *...Then they called the blind man, saying to him, "Be of good cheer. Rise, He is calling you." And throwing aside his garment, he rose and came to Jesus. So Jesus answered and said to him, "What do you want Me to do for you?"...* (Mark 10:49-51)

It was his turn. It was his time. It was his moment. In excitement, Bartimaeus got up, tossed aside his garment, and came over to Jesus. There they stood, face to face. Power locked eyes with blind potential. Jesus was getting ready to start fishing in this man's heart to see if he was ready for the transition. Even though Bartimaeus was blind, Jesus still asked, *"What do you want Me to do for you?"* Why such a question? It should be obvious—right? The man was blind, and he needed to see. Jesus was evaluating whether Blind Bartimaeus actually recognized the moment he was in. Jesus wanted to release potential, but He wanted to make sure that both He and Bartimaeus were on the same page. Jesus didn't want to just touch the guy; He wanted to heal him. Jesus didn't want to pat him on the back and comfort him in the affliction.

There is a chance that the blind man could have responded incorrectly to Jesus' question. He could have given Jesus an answer that revealed a heart not capable of presently carrying a new dimension of glory. He could have simply asked Jesus for a touch—and no more. He could have thrown a pity party, elevating the status of his affliction above the power that Jesus had available to release and unlock Bartimaeus' potential. I know this sounds ridiculous considering who was standing before the blind man, but this example speaks volumes to believers today.

So many of us stand before power and give the wrong answer. We give wrong answers because of how demanding, how outlandish, how supernatural, and how impossible the right ones sound. We give wrong answers because we want to be safe rather than seize the moment in front of us. But if you don't seize it, it will pass you by. I don't care how wild it sounds. If you heard that Jesus had the power to heal blind people and you were Blind Bartimaeus, you would seize that opportunity no matter how "out there" the prospect of a miracle sounded. If you had to stand on your head and turn cartwheels, it wouldn't matter. Power is standing before you, and that power is the only catalyst that can release your potential.

The key is, you have to want it, and that intense want has to exceed your mind's tendency to rationalize. Jesus was familiar with the natural mind. He knew that Bartimaeus might have been in a wrestling match with logic and reason and common sense. "Miracles don't happen." "That's impossible!" "Blind people don't see—they are blind!" We don't know what transpired in his mind. All we know is that he heard Jesus had come into town, and he seized his moment. He knew that regardless how impossible it sounded, Jesus was the only One who could release his potential.

Bartimaeus gave Jesus the correct answer. In responding to Jesus' question, he said, *"Rabbi, I want to see"* (see Mark 10:51 NLT). The result? *"Instantly the man could see, and he followed Jesus down the road"* (Mark 10:52 NLT). It was more than a touch. It was more than a healing. It was more than a miracle or a moment. Bartimaeus was launched into his purpose because he seized his moment, experienced the touch of power, saw potential unleashed, and was propelled into purpose. His ultimate purpose? Although healing was part of his purpose, the end result of his healing was that Bartimaeus could now become one who *followed Jesus.*

REFLECTIONS

1. How should you appropriately respond to the divine moments that God brings into your life? How did Elisha respond?

2. What does it mean to recognize the value of your moment? How will a vision of its value change the way you respond to it?

3. What stands out to you from the example of Blind Bartimaeus—how he responded to his meeting with Jesus?

Chapter 11

NO RETURN TO THE ORDINARY

*And he left the oxen and ran after Elijah, and said,
"Please let me kiss my father and my mother, and then
I will follow you. And he [Elijah] said to him, "Go back
again, for what have I done to you? (1 Kings 19:20)*

Get Messed Up for the Usual

I now want us to look at *what is produced* when power meets potential. Even though it's a brief moment in time, it is a moment that is absolutely pregnant with purpose. Remember, it's the divine intersection of power and potential that bring us into purpose. Your meeting with power is your God-extended invitation into a life that is messed up for everything it used to be.

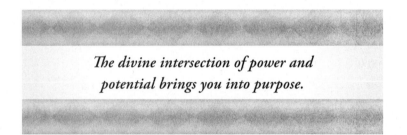

*The divine intersection of power and
potential brings you into purpose.*

Let's rewind a little bit and go back to when Elijah tossed his mantle onto Elisha. The plowman knew what had taken place. It didn't demand a discussion. He knew that the mantle Elijah threw upon him demanded *everything*. This is why he told Elijah that he wanted go back home to kiss his father and mother good-bye. He did not go back home because his heart was still aching for his old season. Elisha went home to say so long and "goodbye" to everything that defined him up until his moment with power.

Likewise, when you have been bleeding for twelve years, and then because of the power you experienced in a single moment the bleeding stops, the mere notion of going back to the bleeding is repulsive. There is nothing back there. Nothing in the plowing. Nothing in the blindness. Nothing in the bleeding. Each of these people experienced a different set of circumstances, but each had a single common denominator—they were invited into a new level. Each one had a collision with power that brought them into a new dimension. Each individual experienced a most unique promotion.

Your promotion makes the plow work of yesterday highly unsatisfying. The very thing that positioned you for promotion can actually rob you of the blessing of promotion if, like Lot's wife, you look back. Jesus tells us to *"Remember Lot's wife"* (Luke 17:32). What's so important about this woman and her decision to look back? As Lot and his family were fleeing the city Sodom and Gomorrah, which the Lord had marked for destruction, they were given a very clear set of instructions: *"Do not look behind you nor stay anywhere in the plain. Escape to the mountains, lest you be destroyed"* (Gen. 19:17). Why? There was nothing back there for them to look at. It was a city in ruins.

Lot and his family had an intersection with power. God paid them a visit in the form of two rescuing angels (see Gen. 19:1). Power was delivering these people out of a dying city. Power pulled them out of a dark place where who they truly were would never be recognized or realized. There was potential inside Lot and his family that remained untapped as long as they remained in the depravity of Sodom. The problem was, something inside Lot's wife was still connected to the old life, the old ways, the old friends, the old places. Something inside her was still deeply attached to how things used to be—so much so that she directly disobeyed the angelic instructions they received. When she looked back, she turned into the very thing that the city became, a *"pillar of salt"* (see Gen. 19:26).

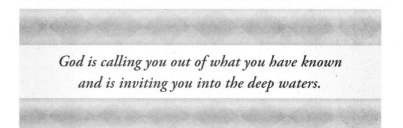

God is calling you out of what you have known and is inviting you into the deep waters.

Maybe Lot's wife thought she could enjoy the best of both worlds. God was calling Lot and his family into the high places. He was calling them up, into the mountains (see Gen. 19:17). Lot's wife was trying to save something that was infinitely inferior to what she was being invited into. In some way, Lot's wife was in bondage to her old life. The prospect of stepping into something new might have been overwhelming. Maybe she was terrified. She had known Sodom. This was her stomping ground. She knew the streets. She knew the city. Maybe she was friends with the neighbors. She knew that Mr.

Jones came out every morning at 8:30 and watered the plants. She knew that Mrs. Jenkins walked the dog after dinner at 6 o'clock. She had a schedule. She had a system. She had a routine. Do you see where I'm going with this? God is calling you out of what you have known and is inviting you into the deep waters. You are being beckoned to abandon the familiar and the comfortable and the safe, and step out into an entirely new dimension of living.

Sadly, many never actually take this step because the familiar and comfortable restrain them.

THE EXTRAORDINARY IS CALLING

So Abram went, as the Lord had told him, and Lot went with him. Abram was seventy-five years old when he departed from Haran. And Abram took Sarai his wife, and Lot his brother's son, and all their possessions that they had gathered, and the people that they had acquired in Haran, and they set out to go to the land of Canaan... (Genesis 12:4-5 NIV).

Sometimes the comfort of an old season tries to keep us from embracing the new thing God wants to launch us into. We prefer the ordinary, because the extraordinary has too much uncertainty attached to it. The ordinary is what we are being invited out of. The ordinary was all fine and good for its time, but now the God of the Extraordinary is calling. Your name is up! Let's not be like Lot's wife who ultimately rejected the summons to step out of her old season. She responded just the opposite of Lot's uncle, Abraham. When his moment came, *Abram went as the Lord had told him* (see Gen. 12:4). He moved toward the unknown and unfamiliar. This was his pathway to promotion.

It's amazing how even if the place where we are living is destructive, like Sodom, or idolatrous like Haran, we still stay because it's familiar. Abram did not, but Lot did. Why? There's comfort in what has become our ordinary. Even if we're blind, even if we're bleeding, some are content to stay in the comfort of their pain instead of stepping forward into the unknown of their purpose. Purpose is only unknown because we have not stepped *in* yet. When power calls us, we must respond, for it's in our response where potential is realized and released.

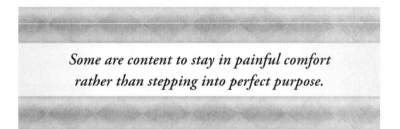

Some are content to stay in painful comfort
rather than stepping into perfect purpose.

For some of us, our pain and problems became a source of perverted comfort because they give us something to fall back on as we are being summoned out into the unknown. Hear me out, I'm not that saying pain, in and of itself, is comfortable. It's not. It stings. It hurts. It restrains. It withholds. It debilitates. It harms. It hinders. Pain is not comfortable; but for some people, they have chosen to identify themselves with their pain. Blind Bartimaeus was recognized as "Blind Bartimaeus." Maybe people identified him by his condition like a nickname. Perhaps this is why Jesus was asking him, "What do you want Me to do for you," when it seemed like his need was quite obvious! But as I mentioned earlier, I think Jesus was searching for something. He wanted to see if this man was really serious, not just about receiving a touch, but getting a name change. Jesus wanted to see how deeply blindness was ingrained in Bartimaeus' identity.

In the same way, Elisha was faced with a choice. His situation was different, although the principle is the same. Even though he was not caught in a debilitating situation, he was nevertheless living at a former level. He was plowing when the invitation to purpose passed him by. Was Elisha going to stay "Elisha the plowman," or would he step into the role of "Elijah the prophet?" Consider the ramifications for just a moment. If Elisha did not respond to the mantle of Elijah and just kept on plowing because plowing is what he knew and plowing was his safety net and plowing was familiar, the prophetic calling assigned to his life would never have been realized. On the other side of each power-filled moment is a release of unlocked potential that completely changes your life. Blind Bartimaeus got healed and became a Christ-follower. Elisha became a prophet who walked in a double portion of the anointing that was upon Elijah. Consider the result of Elisha saying "Yes" to the unknown and unfamiliar.

On the other side of each power-filled moment is a release of unlocked potential that completely changes every life.

Elisha stepped into a realm of miracles that even Elijah had not experienced. These miracles, and the lives they impacted, would have never been realized or demonstrated if Elisha kept on plowing. If he stayed behind in his old realm, in his former glory, in his previous position, he would not have been privileged to participate in the extraordinary exploits that were only activated when he stepped out. If he decided to keep plowing, his eyes would not have seen the Jordan River divided (see 2 Kings 2:14). If he chose to remain a plowman and forfeit his opportunity to become a prophet, he would not have performed a creative miracle that healed the waters at the spring of Jericho (see 2 Kings 2:21).

Understand, all of this potential was available to Elisha. *This* is exactly what was unlocked at the moment of the divine meeting, when Elijah's power awakened Elisha's potential. Maybe his eyes didn't see it all right there when he caught Elijah's mantle. And in your moment of power, you probably won't see the entire plan. Every detail, every stop along the road, every blessing, every meeting, every breakthrough—your mind would not be able to handle it all right there in a single encounter with power. You don't need to know. All you need to understand is that the moment of power activates potential to do things your imagination cannot even conceive.

Second Kings tells us that Elisha went on to miraculously provide oil for the widow woman (4:1-4), raised her son from the dead (4:35), purifies food (4:41), multiplies bread (4:43), heals Naaman's leprosy (5:10), causes a metal ax head to float (6:6), and heals blindness (6:17). Even a dead man is raised to life because his body came into contact with the bones of Elisha (13:21). Even after Elisha was dead, buried, and decayed to the point where only his bones were left, the power upon that man's physical frame was so strong, so potent, that just by coming into contact with it, healing broke out. *This* is what that one moment of power released Elisha to do, both in his life and after he had died.

I wonder what God is getting ready to release inside you!

Yes, in the stepping-out process there is mystery. One moment Elisha was plowing and the next he felt a mantle hit his shoulders. There was mystery in what all of this entailed. Elisha didn't have all the answers. He didn't get some instant download of the complete course of action that would follow his collision with power. He just knew something was shifting. He was ready, he was willing, and in turn he responded. Don't dare settle for the comfort of some old, worn-out season when you are being beckoned and brought into the unknown. It's only unknown because you haven't experienced it yet. You haven't touched it. You haven't tasted it. You haven't smelled it. You haven't seen it. It's unknown because it's not the familiar. It's not the ordinary. It's not what you've always known. It's not where you've been. It's something fresh, something new, and something that's going to shake everything.

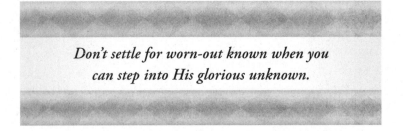

Don't settle for worn-out known when you can step into His glorious unknown.

CHANGE YOUR IDENTITY

The problem for some of us is that the old season, even though it was destructive, is something that we are familiar with, and by continuing to live in that old season of familiar pain, we prevent ourselves from stepping out into the new season of unfamiliar purpose. Somewhere along the line, we identified self with a season.

Good or bad, we cannot identify ourselves by a season, for when the season changes, we get worried. We start shaking. We're nervous. Why? Because who we were is changing. We need to celebrate. If you were Blind Bartimaeus in your former season, I've got good news. You're about to become Healed Bartimaeus. You're about to become Blessed Bartimaeus. You're about to become Bartimaeus, the disciple. Don't ever hold on to some identity you embraced in your former season, because it might have been wrong.

You need to know who you are, absolutely. You need to know who you are and what you have in Christ. You need to know your strengths and weaknesses. You need to be familiar with your faults and foibles. You need to know what you're good at, what you're wired for and how you've been programmed. Those are healthy identities that carry you through any and every season.

There are unhealthy identities like Blind Bartimaeus, when you become identified by your plight or problem. When your addiction labels you. When your bondage becomes a badge. When your name is determined by your enemy.

Embrace the shift. When power meets your potential, God wants to break that false identity and build a fresh one.

Beyond unhealthy identities, there are simply old-season identities you need to deal with. God has called you to be faithful where you are, doing what you're doing—*for now.* Elisha was a plowman, and he faithfully fulfilled this assignment and identity. However, when power unlocked his potential, his profession shifted. His identity changed. What was right yesterday would be wrong today if he tried to continue in that same identity. If Elisha sought to remain *the plowman* while trying to step into his identity as *the prophet,* he would be stepping right into a nervous breakdown. The plowman made it possible for the prophet to emerge. Remember, Elisha was faithful as the plowman and then he was elevated. Promotion was the byproduct of faithfulness in the previous season. But when the moment comes and the mantle hits, you have to think on your feet. Don't hang on to a past identity when God is bringing you into a new present reality.

There are traits of the plowman that will carry over into the prophet. The ability to plow and press and work and toil to break up ground—the very character that the plowman developed in Elisha positioned him to step into his new identity of prophet. These characteristics would continue. They would make the cut. They would endure the transition. Just like who you are—your strengths, your abilities, your knowledge, your skillsets, your wisdom, and your aptitudes. Everything that will keep you moving forward will endure the mantle. Everything from yesterday that will help you step further into today and tomorrow will continue into the your dimension.

At the same time, the stuff that holds you back cannot endure. It cannot go on through. It just can't, as it has no place. You can't let it. Your moment with power exposes you to what can continue—and what cannot. Your glimpse of the next dimension gives you vision for what you can take with you and what you can't take. The only things you can't take are the things that will sabotage your forward momentum.

Just know things aren't going to be like they used to be. Old things might be calling your name, trying to get you to look back. You can't go there. They'll try to convince you that comfortable is better. You just remind them what's on the other side of your unknown and unfamiliar. Elisha stepped into the unknown and unfamiliar and he lived at a new dimension. He walked in a greater anointing. He experienced greater glory. The miracles were greater. He pressed into realms that Elijah never knew.

God has said, *"Behold, the former things have come to pass, and new things I declare; before they spring forth I tell you of them"* (Isa. 42:9). After your meeting with power, you may go back to the same address, but you will not be the same person, because God has done a fresh thing in your life. I repeat, you cannot go back.

> *After meeting with power, you will not be the same person—God has done a fresh thing in you.*

You might try. Elisha did. He tried to go back to his old normal after the meeting, and nothing fit. Nothing made sense. Nothing came close to what he had just received when power passed by. You will go back and look at what you used to call good and say, "What in the world was I thinking?" Whenever God elevates you to the next level, you look at things that you used to call excellent and ask, "What happened to them?" They didn't change. You changed. You received an upgrade. You received a mantle. You were a plower, but now are a prophet. There's nothing wrong with the ox. There's something right with you—you've been exposed to the next level of glory and it's time for you to step on in.

REFLECTIONS

1. Why is it intimidating to leave the ordinary and familiar behind?

2. How is it possible for people to use pain as a source of comfort? How does this prevent you from stepping into the next season?

3. What are the benefits of stepping out into the unknown and unfamiliar?

CHAPTER 12

MAKE FIREWOOD

So Elisha turned back from him, and took a yoke
of oxen and slaughtered them and boiled their
flesh, using the oxen's equipment, and gave it to
the people, and they ate... (1 Kings 19:21).

MAKE FIREWOOD OUT OF THE OLD POSITION

When your potential has awakened it will never rest again. *It will never rest again.* Potential did not orchestrate the meeting with power; it just happened, but since it happened, potential says:

- "I know this is what I've been waiting for all of my life."

- "This is my moment, and I cannot ignore the power to which I have been exposed."

- "I have been plowing on the twelfth yoke of oxen. I cannot go back and assume the family business."

Elisha went back to his home, but did not go back to life on the old level. Even though he physically stood among his family and friends and former living conditions, he was now functioning at the next level. You can live in the next dimension among those who are still in a former level. You are responsible for *you*. You are the one who received the mantle. Trust God's timing and divine orchestration to deal with others who are not living at the level next. You are not God's commissioned constable. You're not His holy law enforcement agent. Your goal is not to make people feel badly about their present level, when you are living in the next. No—you run with what you have. You live at that next level, and the on-looking world will want what you have.

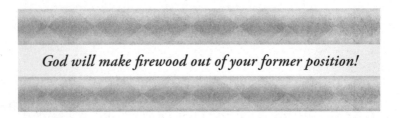

God will make firewood out of your former position!

When Elisha went home, he made a decision. Look at what he does:

> *So Elisha returned to his oxen and slaughtered them.*
> *He used the wood from the plow to build a fire to roast*
> *their flesh...* (1 Kings 19:21 NLT).

The man was serious about moving forward. In this moment, the shift is established. He received the mantle, but he could have gone back home...and stayed. He could have decided that the future was too frightening and succumbed to playing it safe as a plowman, living with Momma and Daddy. The opportunity was obviously there. But Elisha was cut from a different cloth. The man was made of more than that. He was not intimidated by what was before him. He made a decision in his heart that next level living was his only option; and as a result, he took what represented his former life and identity—the oxen and the plow—and broke it up and made firewood out of it.

God is going to make firewood out of your former position! There are things you might be laying down, but there are characteristics and qualities you are upgrading. There is stuff inside of you that's changing its very structure and makeup as you embrace transition. His plow fueled the fire in the same way that what Elisha learned as a plowman surely contributed to the fire God used to release upon the earth through him. This was Elisha's past. He was a plowman, and that plow became the fire that destroyed the option of going back to yesterday, but a fire that fueled his forward momentum into tomorrow. Elisha's past was his profession. Even though the ox became dinner and the plow became firewood, the things that Elisha gleaned through being a plowman were set ablaze in the fire of surrender. In the same way that Moses threw down his shepherd's rod before the Lord and it was anointed to accomplish the supernatural (see Exod. 4:1-4), so Elisha throws down what he has—the ox and the plow—and it becomes the fire that launches him into the next glory.

FUEL FOR THE NEXT GLORY

God doesn't want to destroy you; He wants to elevate you. A rod in Moses' hand could only accomplish natural things. He could lead sheep. That was Moses' ordinary. That was what he had known and that was his realm of familiarity. God was not looking to take away his shepherd's staff; He was looking to touch it with power and release potential. Let's look at Moses' story, for it illustrates what is going on with Elisha.

> *So the Lord said to him, "What is that in your hand?"*
> *He said, "A rod." And He said, "Cast it on the ground."*
> *So he cast it on the ground, and it became a serpent...*
> (Exodus 4:2-3).

The same God is asking you, "What is that in your hand?" Are you still clinging to the plow of yesterday while trying to live in a new dimension? God doesn't want to snatch your plow away. He doesn't want to steal your shepherd's rod. He's not on some quest to make your life miserable and take all of your stuff away. No, He wants to make the devil miserable by getting you to hand your stuff over to Him, and let Him infuse it with power. He wants to ignite what you have. The key is yielding it to Him. If He sets the plow on fire while you are holding it, it's going to hurt. It's going to burn. If you don't let go, and the fire consumes it, you will die. You won't be able to sustain the fire. It will kill you, not promote you.

God doesn't set a plow on fire while it is still in the care of the plowman; in the same way, He doesn't turn rods into serpents while they are still being held by the shepherds. Why? Because if we are unwilling to submit these things to God, we are unable to sustain what He wants to release through them.

God wants to take the very things that define your position and profession, and set them on fire.

God wants to take the very things that define your position and profession, and set them on fire. That's living in a new dimension. It can be shocking because it's so different. Moses was shocked when his shepherd's rod turned into a serpent. In Exodus 4:3, Moses watches the supernatural transformation of staff to snake, and we read that *"Moses fled from it."* We've already covered this ground. We cannot become intimidated by the next level of glory. God is taking things we were comfortable with and charging them with supernatural power. Skills we had in the old season are being touched by His power. Potential's coming out that we didn't know was there. It shocks us. We're frightened. At times, we want to run away. The whole thing is too glorious, and a bit too much.

But you can't go back.

The plow's burning. The ox is dead and cooked. People are eating its flesh. You've gone too far and there is no reversing it. Keep going. The same staff that scared Moses saved the nation of Israel. The rod that led sheep was the same rod that led God's chosen people out of bondage. God's taking your old position and setting it on fire. Moses led sheep in the wilderness in one level; but in the next, he led people in the wilderness. Elisha plowed the ground in one dimension; but in the next, he plowed the soil of human hearts to receive the seed of God's prophetic word. I dare you to get excited about God taking what you had in your previous level and empowering it in a new level.

Make Firewood Out of Your Past

Elisha's plow was not only his position and profession, it also symbolized his past. This is what he had known and had been defined by. He was Elisha the plowman. We've already talked about the need to leave the past behind, move forward, and refuse to look back. I want to take it a step further. I want to take this opportunity to encourage you that the same God who sets fire to your profession and position can also set fire to your past. It's one thing to talk about how God uses our talents and our giftings and our accolades and our triumphs—it's another thing to talk about how He uses our past. And I'm not talking about your past a school teacher, your past as a dentist, your past as a construction worker, your past as a taxi driver, your past as the star quarterback for the high school football team. It's easy to accept that He uses these things because they are noteworthy and safe.

> *The same God who sets fire to your profession and position can also set fire to your past.*

I don't want to play it safe and keep it cute. I don't want to talk about the good stuff; I want us to get into the grit. It's one thing to believe God uses your past successes—it's another level of thinking that emboldens us to believe that He wants to use our past failures, messes, mistakes, shortcomings, train wrecks, disgraces, shame, and sins. When power hits potential, we run—we don't argue. We don't argue with power, giving it every reason why we shouldn't be called. You know how people give God their reasons, "But God, don't You know who I am? Don't You know what I've done?" Power comes; and instead of embracing it, we resist it. We remind power that our past disqualifies us for the present calling. We try to persuade power that we are unworthy of the summons because in our past we feel like we have squandered our potential.

Let me remind you, God is not a man and does not operate according to how we think He should work. Your past does not intimidate Him. We remind God of our past as if He is clueless about what happened. When He summons us, it is absolutely ridiculous to start reminding Him why He should *not* be calling us. He knows what He's doing. He's not blind. He's seen our faults. He sees our struggles. Those things done in the darkness that no one else knows about. God saw them, and still loves you. Those memories that bring you shame every time you invite them back into your mind. God was there. He was there in the darkness, and He was there in the light. He was there when you were with the person you shouldn't have been with, and He was there when you weren't in the place you should have been. He was there in the pit, and He was there in the palace. He was there when you lied. He was there when you cheated. He was there when you prepared your taxes. He was there when you lost your mind. He was there when you crossed the line. He saw every moment, still loves you, and is still summoning you. Don't insult Him by asking, "Why me?"

None of us deserve anything. We didn't go looking for grace; grace came banging down our door. We're not good enough for God. Nothing inside of us cried out for God to come and rescue us; He put the cry inside. That's all true. Paul says it best:

And you were dead in the trespasses and sins in which you once walked, following the course of this world, following the prince of the power of the air, the spirit that is now at work in the sons of disobedience—among whom we all once lived in the passions of our flesh, carrying out the desires of the body and the mind, and were by nature children of wrath, like the rest of mankind (Ephesians 2:1-3 ESV).

This is our past. If anyone had a problem past, it was the apostle Paul. He persecuted and killed believers. He was a murderer. He was the worst of the worst. He recognized this, writing of himself, *"I am the least of the apostles, who am not worthy to be called an apostle, because I persecuted the church of God"* (1 Cor. 15:9).

Paul had a past. Maybe you had a past. Does this exclude you from the present purpose of God? No. Even after Paul gives us the list in Ephesians 2, reminding us of every bad, wretched, and unspeakable thing we have done, we are invited into a new present and a new future. God is not blind to our former trespasses. He watched as we walked in league with the devil, doing his bidding. He saw as we made passions and lusts our gods and idols. We think the next verse should be a disqualifier, when in fact it simply reads, *"But God..."* (Eph. 2:4). These two words are your invitation to live in a new reality where your past is not counted against you.

Paul continues:

But God, being rich in mercy, because of the great love with which he loved us, even when we were dead in our trespasses, made us alive together with Christ—by grace you have been saved—and raised us up with him and seated us with him in the heavenly places in Christ Jesus" (Ephesians 2:4-6 ESV).

Power brought you into a whole new dimension of living. Your present and your future are not dictated by your past. In fact, God uses your past as a tool of measurement. Your past reminds you how far He's brought you and how deep you've gone. This is how power makes firewood of out the past. When you view your past in light of your present summons, your heart is ignited. You can't shut down the thanksgiving. You know you're not worthy, but He called you worthy. Of course you're not deserving, but God said you are deserving. The King is calling. The courier is handing you the royal invitation. Don't hide your face. Don't run off into the shadows in shame. Stand tall. Remember where you came from, but feel the fire of where He's bringing you.

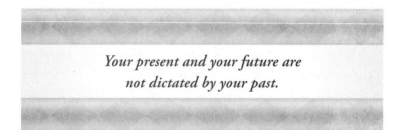

Your present and your future are
not dictated by your past.

If you don't have a past, you don't have the fire. I believe God wants to take your past and make firewood out of it. It will be the flame that ignites your future, sets off your destiny, creates your passion for your purpose, and releases you into another dimension. The past brings everything into perspective.

Set the ox on fire. Turn that ox into food and feed the neighborhood. Elisha might have said, "This can feed you, but it can't feed me. I cannot continue to follow a dumb thing. I know I've got some more rows to be plowed, but I cannot stay in my position, for the traditions of men will make the Word of God of no affect. If I continue to stay in the sensible circle, making the acceptable motions, trying to live up to the status quo, I am going to miss my moment. So here, you eat it. It's not that it is bad. It was good for me at one time—but a shift has occurred."

REFLECTIONS

1. How can you make firewood out of your position or profession? How does it provide fuel for your next level?

2. What does it mean to make firewood out of your past?

3. How should you respond to your past when God summons you into your future?

CHAPTER 13

LIVE ON A NEW LEVEL

...Then he [Elisha] arose and followed Elijah,
and became his servant (1 Kings 19:21).

DISCOVER WHO YOU BECAME

No longer shall your name be called Abram, but your
name shall be Abraham; for I have made you a father
of many nations (Genesis 17:5).

In the same way that Abram received a divine name change
to Abraham, Elisha experienced a similar transformation. Elisha returned from burning the plow and feeding the ox to the
townsmen, and stepped right into the flow of his next level. We
read that Elisha, *"arose and followed Elijah, and became his servant"* (1 Kings 19:21). Note the word *became*.

Elisha was not dating a new dimension. He wasn't flirting
with it. He wasn't testing out the waters. He wasn't satisfied
with a touch of power that made him feel good, but didn't
transform his life. The result of Elisha's meeting with Elijah? Power awakened potential, and potential was unleashed.
Elisha stepped into his new identity. He *became* Elijah's servant. He didn't walk with Elijah for a little while, get tired,

and then go back to plow and cook oxen with the folks back home. Home was redefined for Elisha. "Plan B" was removed from his equation. His only option was moving forward with Elijah, because when you become something, it's difficult to un-become it.

When you *do* something, you can stop doing it. Elisha could have *done* the whole serving thing for Elijah, but then turned back when things stopped making sense. When Elijah got too cranky, Elisha could have said, "This is not for me. I don't want to deal with you and your temper and your craziness and your strangeness. I'm out, I'm through. I served for a season, but now I'm going back." There's no going back to something for someone who *became* something.

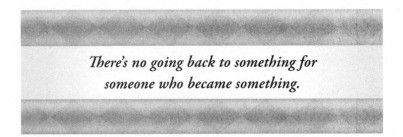

There's no going back to something for someone who became something.

When the teacher was taken up in the flaming chariots, Elisha could have turned back and run for his life. "I didn't sign up for this. I wasn't planning on this taking place. Nobody warned me. Nobody told me what was coming. I want out." If Elisha chose to simply serve Elijah as an act, it would have been easier for him to turn back. But Elisha's encounter with power didn't just sustain him for a season. His DNA was changed. The plowman started to become a prophet when he *became* Elijah's servant.

THE LOW PERSON IN A NEW LEVEL

And whoever exalts himself will be humbled, and he who humbles himself will be exalted (Matthew 23:12).

Somebody might say, "Well Elisha, you're still following." He says, "Yeah, but I'm following on a whole other level." He wasn't following an ox, he was following a prophet. What he was following before was the family business. He was following the trajectory of his history. Now he was following in the direction of his destiny. The same is true for you. Don't get discouraged if the encounter with power has you still following something or someone. Following is not the problem; it's what or who you are following that determines at what level you choose to live. Was Elisha going to keep following an animal around, or was he going to follow Elijah?

> *I'd rather be the low man in my destiny than the lead man in my history.*

Elisha did not mind following. Why? When you're following at a new level, everything's different. I'd rather be the low man in my destiny than the lead man in my history. You know what I'm talking about. That moment comes when we're invited into a new level, and what happens? We look back at what *was,* because what *was* kept us in a high position. But where was that high position? Elisha's "high position" was following around an ox and plowing. Elisha's position might have been high in his old season; but now, he was invited into a whole new dimension of living. He was exposed to a realm of reality beyond his current living conditions. Yes, he was going to have to start at the bottom, following Elijah, but I'd rather follow Elijah into my purpose any day than stay around in some worn-out season that holds nothing else for me.

The same is true for you.

Don't get discouraged if you keep following into your new season. Think about it. You're not following an ox anymore, you're following Elijah. You're following the person or the thing or the opportunity or the business or the career or the idea or the path that is taking you into the next level. You see, the season of the ox prepared Elisha for living at the next level, but it would never bring him into the next level. Where you were, before your meeting with power, had its purpose—in its season. Your old season made sense *before* power came walking by. But it makes no sense for us to choose to remain in the old season. I don't care if you're the prince in your old season when power pays a visit, because the pauper in the new season is leagues ahead of the prince in an old season.

Now, you're going to come in on the bottom level of a new dimension. Up until this point, everybody in your life has been pulling after you, looking to you for answers, looking for solutions, calling you about this, and calling you about that because you were the plower of the twelfth yoke of oxen. That was your identity in the old season. You were large and in charge. You felt special. You had the answers. You knew the solutions. You had it all figured out.

But don't be afraid. In the new season, you're going to start out knowing nothing, and I'd rather know nothing in the new than keep on knowing everything in the old. You're carrying what you learned in the old season into the new season. God's not erasing your memory. The key is, you're stepping into the unfamiliar and unknown. Celebrate it. Every step you take toward where you don't have a clue where you're going, be confident that you are walking farther toward your purpose. Your potential is being released. You're taking significant strides toward fulfilling destiny.

HOW TO WALK IN THE DARK

For we walk by faith, not by sight (2 Corinthians 5:7).

We throw around phrases like, "Walk by faith, not by sight." In church, when the preacher talks about this truth, we shout "Amen," and get excited; but when everything changes and we start walking in the dark, we cannot depend on sight. What you've seen has not prepared you for where you're going. What you saw in the old season won't help you as you begin navigating your new dimension. If Elisha tried to see life from a plowman's perspective in his new season, he would have been lost. He didn't know from what perspective he would be seeing. The terrain was alien. All he knew was this guy passed by him, tossed his mantle upon his shoulders, and kept on going. Using what sense he had, Elisha had to assume that this prophet who passed by and kept on walking *knew* where he was going. Elisha didn't know where Elijah was going, but Elijah looked like he knew. In turn, Elisha followed the leader.

Faith is your anchor and sustainer in the new season. Faith that the One who called us is faithful (see 1 Thess. 5:24). Faith that our steps are ordered by the Lord (see Ps. 37:23). Faith helps you see in the dark. And when you feel like you can't see, faith steadies your heart to trust what you know. What is true. What is constant. What is unchanging. What is invisible. Faith is the only way we are able to see in the dark of transition.

> *Faith is the only way we are able to*
> *see in the dark of transition.*

Earlier on, we studied how your meeting with power transitions you into a realm of unfamiliarity and un-knowability. You don't know where you're going because it's unfamiliar. It's unfamiliar because you've never been there. Now, I want to help you learn how to walk in the dark. That's what living at a new level is like. You're walking forward. You may not see where you're going, but you know that you're walking. You put one foot in front of the other. Things aren't clear. They don't make sense. You may trip and fall. There's even a good chance you're going to fail and make mistakes. That's okay. It's legal. I'd choose failure in a new dimension over success in an old season that's passed me by. Think about it. Success in an old season actually does not move you forward into your destiny and purpose. If you choose to stay behind in the old and settle for success as a plower, when you're really called to be a prophet, you could be the most successful plower there is, but your purpose as a prophet is still waiting for you to step up.

You're going into a new dimension, living at a new level. With it comes a level of uncertainty, a level of humility, a level where you have to learn and you have to grow and you have to pray and you have to read. This will be unfamiliar territory. For all of your life, up until now, you have been operating in the familiarity of your comfort zone. You do the same things over and over again, following the routine that you always knew. You had the field mapped out and knew every corner and every crevice. You understood it. You knew where the rocks were. You knew where the roots were. You knew where the snakes hid. You knew where the opposition was. You knew where everything was. Your life was defined by the old system and old cycle. But ever since power hit, your potential is coming out and it demands something new. The old wineskin can't contain what's about to break forth in your life.

BREAK THE CYCLE

...but one thing I do, forgetting those things which are behind and reaching forward to those things which are ahead (Philippians 3:13).

I want you to proactively pursue discomfort. You read this right—don't adjust your eyes. This is what Paul was saying in Philippians 3:13. He had a lot to rest on. He had his education. He had his theological pedigree. He had his affluence and influence. All of those things were in his past. They represented his old level. How does he respond? He chooses to forget what was in the past and presses and reaches and pushes into the things which are ahead. This is the key to breaking the old cycles associated with the old season—simply starting new ones.

For so many people, comfort is an idol. It's only when you step out of your comfort zone that you can start learning how to navigate the unfamiliar terrain of your new season. Paul was a Pharisee turned preacher of the Gospel. He was an academic turned traveling evangelist. He was ushered into a dimension of living he had never conceived of, and yet he preferred to press toward the glorious unknown than choose to rest in his pampered past. He knew that what was ahead was greater than what was behind.

> **When you step out of your comfort zone, you will learn how to navigate in your new season.**

I pray that this releases a stirring in your spirit that what's in your future, what's ahead and on the horizon is overwhelmingly superior to what was behind, even if what was behind appeared to be a benchmark. Too many of us get stuck in old cycles because we put limits on God. We limit what He can do with our potential. We think that the old life and all its trimmings was as good as it gets. God wants to bust apart your idea of what "as good as it gets" looks like. You haven't dreamed of what God can do. You can't comprehend what's up ahead. Your mind cannot begin to fathom what the Almighty has on the other side of your new season. I declare to you, according to the Word of God, that *"Eye has not seen, nor ear heard, nor have entered into the heart of man the things which God has prepared for those who love Him"* (1 Cor. 2:9). That statement alone is grounds for a shout, but don't stop there.

We look at verses like this, get a spiritual high, and then go right back to our cycle. Why? Because we isolate ourselves from the incomparable, unimaginable things God wants to bring into our lives. This verse wows us, showing what God wants to do, and yes, even has prepared *"for those who love Him,"* but look at what Paul adds in the following verse—*"But God has revealed them to us through His Spirit"* (v. 10). Right here we discover that even though we're stepping into new dimensions, there is a promise that we will *not* always have to walk in the dark. The Spirit of the living God dwells inside you. The One who searches and knows the mind of God, the deep things of His heart, dwells in you and tells you where to go (see 1 Cor. 2:10-12, 3:16; John 16:13). He directs your footsteps. He gives you wisdom. He releases understanding. He brings clarity. You have not been left alone as an orphan—God Himself has come to live inside you as the Holy Spirit (see John 14:18). Yes, you will walk through the dark, but you will not walk through the dark of a new season alone because God is always with you. God is in you. God is for you. God is in your corner.

I believe the Lord is saying to you, "The cycle has been broken over your life!" It's completely broken. You're never going to be the same. How you used to do things will not define how you do them in your next dimension. You're going to speak differently. You're going to stand differently. You're going to teach differently. You're going to run numbers differently. You're going to sing differently. You're going to practice medicine differently. You're going to raise your kids differently. You're going to love your spouse differently. Everything's different because it's a new dimension!

REFLECTIONS

1. What's the difference between doing and becoming?

2. How is it a good thing to be the "low person at a new level?"

3. Describe what it looks like to walk in the dark. How have you experienced this in your life?

CHAPTER 14

THE FINAL TESTS

And he [Elijah] said to him, "Go back again, for
what have I done to you?" (1 Kings 19:20).

In this last chapter, I want to give with some practical tools that
will help you identify whether or not you are living in alignment
with your new level. When you get there, you need to stay there.
Remember, you're changed. You're a new man. A new woman.
Elisha *became* Elijah's servant. One of the worst things that we
can experience is living out of alignment with our new level.
Why? It produces purposelessness. You will always be making
strides toward fulfilling your purpose as you live in alignment
with your level.

Here are some simple tests that will help you recognize
whether or not you are living in the place that power promoted
you into.

THE ROOM TEST

First, we have the *room test*. I always say that if you are the
smartest person in a room, you are in the wrong room. Get out!
You are too big for that room. Think about it for a minute. If

you are going to live at another level, you need to always be learning. You need to always be progressing. There's always something to read. There's always a seminar to watch or listen to. There's always room for development. I'm not saying become a workaholic. What I am inviting you into is a process. Process means there is room to grow.

> *If you are the smartest person in a room,*
> *you are in the wrong room. Get out!*

Elisha might have been the smartest guy in town—or at least the smartest when it came to what he knew. But everything changed when Elijah came by. The master plower was touched by the master prophet, and now the guy's whole identity shifted. The master quickly became the apprentice. This is truly the test of whether or not you are living in alignment with your new level. If you continue to seek out places where you are the smartest person in the room, you need to find some new rooms. Pursue some different influences. Find people who challenge you and draw out your potential.

THE WOMB TEST

Most assuredly, I say to you, unless one is born again,
he cannot see the kingdom of God (John 3:3).

Second, is the *womb test*. If you want to *see* at a new level, you are going to have to be born again. In the same way you needed to experience a birthing process to see the Kingdom of God, you need to be reborn in order to see your new dimension of living. We are going to stay here a little bit longer, as I believe if you truly get this, you will never try to squeeze back into an old season again.

If where you currently are cannot fit you anymore, you need to be born. You need to come out. It is like a mother who is ready to give birth. I believe this is where you were when power passed by. Elisha was ready for transition, and all it took was a push from Elijah to turn the plowman into a prophet in training.

The womb got too small to hold you, and you needed to come out. You needed to make a transition from the womb to the room. You needed to get out of a small place and step into a larger place. You might have been the largest person in that womb, but now, on the outside, you feel like the smallest person in the new world. That means you've graduated to a new level. Now it's time for you to grow. It is time to develop. It's time to learn how to say "Ma-Ma" and "Da-Da."

That womb is too small to hold you. You've outgrown it, and the discomfort that exists is between the womb and the infant. It is painful to the mother and it is painful to the baby when you have outgrown the space you have been in. The only choice you have is to be born. Your only option is to come out. This is what happened when power met potential, and Elijah gave Elisha his mantle. That was the push Elisha's potential needed to come forth.

Can you imagine if, along the way, Elisha turned around and tried to go back to his old way of living? Sometimes that happens. Even though we've been born, and we have become a new person at a new level, we can get distracted by old level stuff. Old level situations. Old level places. Old level people. Old level activities. We try to participate, but they hurt. Why? It's like a two-year-old trying to go back into the mother's womb. It's just painful. It doesn't work. It doesn't look right. It makes no sense. The baby doesn't belong there.

How are you feeling right now?

YOU ARE BREAKING OUT

Are there things in your life that are to squeeze you back into your former level? It won't work. It can't. You're new. Elisha was a prophet, not a plowman. You're a new person on a new course living at a new level. If you feel the strain and the pain of being pushed back into the womb, get out of those situations. That's not where you belong. The same was true for Nicodemus in John 3. The man was not like the Sanhedrin court that he came from. You are not like your background. How do I know you're not one of *them?* Because you see on a whole other level. Nicodemus perceived something about this Man Jesus that none of his colleagues and peers were pressing into. Nicodemus was in transition. He recognized something about Jesus that his cohorts did not understand. He could not convince them because he has been birthed into a new dimension, and they were still operating at the old one.

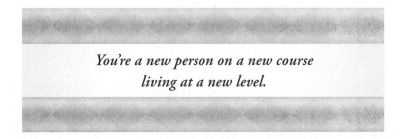

You're a new person on a new course
living at a new level.

It was time for the teacher to become a student again. Nicodemus was *"a ruler of the Jews"* (John 3:1). He was a leader and an authority. He had power and position. His old level was full of prestige among his people. But there was a problem—the water had broken over his life. He met power. Something was happening inside him. He started to see at a new level.

I want to announce to you that the water has broken over your life. You will have to be fed on another level. You're not going to get nourishment through the cord from which you used to receive food. You are going to have to take more responsibility for your food. You cannot just live from sermon to sermon.

In the past, the Lord fed you manna falling down into your tent, but now you're coming into your promised land. Prepare your victuals; for in three days you will cross this Jordan. You are coming into another dimension. You have got to begin to feed on another level. Learn on another level. Read on another level. Interact with people on another level. Parent on another level. Run a household on another level. Build a business on another level. Treat patients on another level. Everything is upgraded.

You have got to get out of that womb. And if you are already out, don't go back there. Don't be drawn back to a place that won't fit you. Don't be enticed by those rooms where you are the know-it-all. Deep down, you know you've got to get out. You've got to get out of this rut. You've got to get rid of that plow. You've got to burn the ox.

POTENTIAL'S FINAL TEST

Potential, here is your final test. Elijah says to Elisha, *"go back home."* We have looked at that process already, where Elisha returns home, deals with the townsmen, prepares them a meal, burns his plow, and moves onward. We have already gone through all of that. Now I want us to look at the test of discouragement. This is the last test Elisha needs to pass before he moves forward.

> *You cannot earn the right to lead until you pass the test of discouragement.*

You cannot earn the right to lead until you pass the test of discouragement. If I can talk you out of it, you are not the one for the new level. Elijah tried out this test on Elisha to see what the plowman was made of, to see if he really was the one. Yes, he caught the mantle. Yes, he ran up to Elijah. Obviously, he knew he got something within him. He recognized that power touched something. Here is the true test. Will your realized potential survive discouragement? Look at how Elijah responded to the excited Elisha. He looked at him and said, *"Go back again, for what have I done to you?"* (1 Kings 19:20). This wasn't nice. It did not sound affirming at first. The one who brought power that called forth potential was now telling Elisha to go back home.

More than anything, Elijah was looking to see how Elisha would respond. Would he get bent out of shape? Would he go home and not return? Would Elijah's harsh attitude push the plowman away? How much did Elisha really want his new level? The test had been given. How would Elisha respond?

How will you respond?

Will you keep moving forward if things do not unfold the way you think they should? Will you keep following even if you get offended? Upset? If someone talks to you harshly? If someone corrects you? If somebody criticizes you? If others point fingers and laugh at you? Will you keep moving forward if you forget why you were doing this to begin with? *What got into me? Why am I going in this direction? I can't see at this new level. It's all foreign. It's all unfamiliar. At least in the old level I knew where everything was. I knew how everything worked. Everything made sense.* What will you follow? These thoughts are not unusual; they aren't bad. They are entirely normal. They are the common assault upon everyone who is invited into a new dimension.

The test is passed or failed in how you *respond* to the thoughts and feelings and temptations and persecutions and offenses. You don't fail if you feel. You don't fail if you think. You don't fail if you catch yourself asking why. You don't fail if your mind starts trying to make sense of what you're doing and where you're going. These things do not determine your grade. It is what you do that determines where you go. The next level has to be that real to you. That necessary. It has got to become so real to you that you cannot breathe without it.

THE NEXT-BREATH TEST

A young preacher saw an old retired preacher who had a massive, huge, anointed ministry. The old preacher was fishing down by the riverbed. This young preacher approached the old preacher and said to him, "I hate to bother you, but this is my opportunity. I may never get this chance again, and I want to minister under the same kind of glory that you minister under." The old man didn't even look up at him. He kept on fishing. The young preacher started to walk away, and he thought to himself, *I may never have this chance again.* He said, "Mr., I hate to bother you, but I can't walk away. I may never get this chance again, and I want to minister under the anointing that you minister under."

And the old man kept on fishing. And the young man kept bothering him and bothering him and bothering him. Finally the old man put down the fishing rod, got up on his feet and snatched the young guy by his neck. He picked him up and threw him into the water. The young man couldn't swim. He couldn't swim in that dimension, so he started going down in it and coming up again. "Help!" he cried. He went down under the water again, and then popped back up, "Help!" Up and down he went, all the while crying out for help.

Finally the old man reached down into the water, stretched forth his hand, and snatched the young man out of the water. The young preacher was panting. He was gasping for air. He was confused and crying. "But I don't understand. I respected you. I admired you, and you picked me up and threw me into the water. I can't swim." The old man looked at him and said, "You remember that last time when you came up out of the water?" The young man was still catching his breath, "Of course, I remember. I can't forget it." He said, "You remember how badly you wanted that next breath?" He said, "Of course I remember. If I didn't get another breath, I was going to die." The old preacher said, "That's how badly you have to want it. You have to want it like you want your next breath. When you want it like that, then you're ready."

You have got to walk into that next level like you need your next breath of air. You are not playing with it. It's not some game. When you want purpose badly enough to do whatever it takes to get there—to control your passions, your foolishness, and your craziness to get there—that is when you're ready to step into it.

Purpose awaits the ready. God's not playing hide and seek with your purpose. He's looking for those who are actually serious about stepping into what they've been designed to do.

> *God's not playing hide and seek with your purpose. He's looking for those who are serious about stepping into their destiny.*

When you're ready to stay up and study while other people play games to get there, then you're ready. Nobody's going to give you purpose on credit. Nobody's going to give it to you because you look cute. You have to pay the price to operate in the next dimension, and after you've suffered awhile, and after you've been talked about a while, and after you've faced all kinds of discouragement and come through all kinds of hell and say, "I still want it," then God says, "I'm going to release another wave of glory in your life."

If you want it, you have got to run after it. Not walk. Not slug. Not wade. Not shuffle. Not jig. Not dance. You've got to run into it and run with it. Elisha got the mantle and ran toward Elijah. He could have gotten discouraged when Elijah told him to go back. But he didn't. He thought, *Go back...to what? I've got nothing to go back to. I've been ruined and wrecked for anything I could possibly go back to. Forward's the only option. That's the only route I want to travel.* The pace has changed. You almost drowned several times. You nearly died several times. You almost went completely under—but there was something down inside that kept you fighting your way back up again.

Because of your potential, because of the purpose you have been marked for, He did not let the waters drown you. He said, *"When you pass through the waters, I will be with you; and through the rivers, they shall not overflow you. When you walk through the fire, you shall not be burned, nor shall the flame scorch you. For I am the Lord your God"* (Isa. 43:2-3). The Lord your God is with you. He was with you through the past, He is with you in the present, and He will be with you for the future. He is not leaving or changing, for He says, *"For I am the Lord, I do not change"* (Mal. 3:6).

Anybody else would have drowned in the hell you went through. Anybody else would have died in it. Anybody else would have lost their mind. Anybody else would have had a nervous breakdown, but you kept fighting your way back up to the top. And now there is a glory that God is going to release on your life. Don't be mistaken, it has to be released on the extraordinary. Not the perfect. Not the all-cleaned-up. Not the goodie-two-shoes. Extraordinary is the one willing to do whatever it takes to walk in the new dimension.

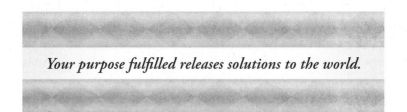

Your purpose fulfilled releases solutions to the world.

It cannot be released on people who haven't been over their heads, almost went under, nearly collapsed, almost fainted, and almost lost their minds. You are the future. Your purpose fulfilled releases solutions to this world. A double portion is at your disposal. Just when you thought you had it all, God says, "I'm taking you higher. I'm about to blow your mind." If you thought the last level was the best, I've got good news for you—your eye has not seen, nor has your ear heard, nor has your heart even imagined of what God is bringing you into.

REFLECTIONS

1. What is the room test? The womb test?

2. How have you experienced either one of these tests in your life? What did they look like?

3. What does the next-breath test look like to you? How have you experienced this one?

AN IMPARTATION

Then the hand of the Lord came upon
Elijah... (1 Kings 18:46).

Now to Him who is able to do exceedingly abundantly
above all that we ask or think, according to the
power that works in us (Ephesians 3:20).

In our final moments together, I don't want you to simply close this book, put it on a shelf, and go back to living life as usual. I hope you received some good information; but most of all, I want to see you experience impartation. I want these pages to serve as your escort into the next level, your new dimension. I pray the Spirit of God whetted your appetite for new realms of glory, anointing, potential, and power that you didn't even know were inside of you. They were waiting, just locked up inside of you, for a collision with power.

So here is my prayer for you—that the powerful hand of the Lord would come upon you, even now while you read these words. As the hand of the Lord was upon Elijah, and the hand of the Lord was upon Elisha, was upon Moses, and the hand of the Lord was upon Joshua, I pray that you experience this same touch of power that launches you into your new dimension. Into your new season. Into your new level.

I pray that the powerful hand of the Lord would be upon every area of your life. Not one gift or talent remains untouched. Not one ounce of potential misses out. The hand of the Lord is upon your house. The hand of the Lord is upon your business. The hand of the Lord is upon your ministry. The hand of the Lord is on your family. The hand of the Lord is on your schooling. The hand of the Lord is on your finances. The hand of the Lord is on your past. The hand of the Lord is on your future. The hand of the Lord is upon *you*.

So let this be your prayer:

> *Lord, whatever You are doing in the earth right now, don't do it without me. Touch me with Your power. Orchestrate the divine appointments. Bring me into collision with destiny-defining moments. Give me eyes to see what You are doing. Ears to hear You speaking. And a heart that responds to how You are moving in my life. I run toward everything You have for me, not looking back. Thank You, Father, for bringing me into my purpose.*

This is what happens when power meets potential.

CHAPTER 1

PURPOSE AND POWER

And we know that all things work together for good to them that love God, to them who are the called according to His purpose (Romans 8:28).

───══════───

When we look at the course of our lives, it sometimes appears to be a chaotic path. The course seems to have no certain direction. Yes, even Christians often find themselves questioning the meaning and course of their lives. The things that God does in our lives, and the incidents and situations that happen in many instances, appear to be a haphazard, erratic display of a madman who gets pleasure from seeing his subjects suffer and live in despair.

But with God, this is not the case. There is a reason to the riddle. There is an answer to the question, clarity to the confusion, and calmness in the chaos. A bright new day dawns after the dark night. There is a time and a purpose to everything under the sun, a method to the madness.

Knowing God's divine purpose for your life is one of the greatest assets and enablements to help understand and make sense of the perplexities and complications that seem to overwhelm. People who possess such knowledge possess power. Jesus displayed an assurance of knowing His purpose in life and ministry. When people sought to kill Him for His stand and boldness in declaring the truth, He didn't get fearful and back down from what He had said. No! Jesus stood His ground. Why? He knew His purpose. His purpose was to destroy the works of the devil, not be destroyed by the works of the devil. (See First John 3:8.)

POWER

Jesus stood His ground!

LIVING

When you are assured of your purpose, you're not fearful of men or external personal conflicts that attempt to hinder you. Why? Because you know with confidence that sooner or later every trial, every hindering situation, and every opposing person and thing in your life will eventually and inevitably bow and submit to God's plan and purpose for your life. It's just a matter of time and circumstance.

The person who knows his or her purpose and God-given vision behaves in a strategic, precise, and decisive manner for spiritual warfare. Paul told Timothy to wage a good warfare by the prophecies that went before him (see 1 Tim. 1:18). When you know your purpose, you won't sit and passively allow things to occur that are contrary to God's purpose and vision for your life. Neither will you be so quick to get discouraged when situations bring conflict and disorder to your life. You know *all* things are working together for your good, because you love the Lord and are called according to His purpose. You don't become frustrated or overwhelmed by those things you can't pray away, rebuke away, cast away, fast away, confess away, or speak away. Why? Because you know that if it's in your life, God has allowed it and He wants to use it (since it's there) to transform you into the express image of Christ. He will bring you into that purpose for which you were created. *All* things, not some, work together for the good of those who love the Lord.

POWER

All things work together for good for those who love the Lord.

LIVING

Therefore, if you are confused, ready to give up, wondering what's going on and what all the turmoil and chaos you're experiencing is about, ask God, "Why?" He just might say, "It's about purpose." Maybe He's building a foundation of character in your life. Perhaps it will enable you to obtain the success and blessing that is to be poured into your life. Maybe it is a prelude to the powerful anointing that is about to come upon you.

He's got to teach you how to trust Him now, while you are in the desert, so that when you get into the Promised Land and people start acting funny toward you because they're jealous of the anointing on your life, you won't be afraid to cut the ungodly tie. You know your help comes not from others, but from the Lord. Do you understand what I'm saying? I know you do. If you don't, you'd better ask somebody! But don't just ask anybody, ask the Lord! Call on the Lord and He will answer you. Go ahead. Don't be afraid. Ask Him, "Lord, why?"

POWER

There is a purpose and reason for your life!

LIVING

Why is there so much strain, why so much struggle, so much conflict, why so much hell? Could it be because I am a man or woman of destiny? Could it be because there's a purpose, a reason for my life? Am I going through so much because I was not brought into this earth haphazardly, but because there is actually some divine, ordained logic to my being? Is it true that I'm not some mistake my mother and father made one night in the heat of passion or uncontrollable lust? (If you were born out of wedlock or even as a result of rape, you're not an illegitimate child. What your parents did was illegitimate—you are not. You need to know that as truth.)

You may wonder: *God, is it possible that You have a divine motive, a divine reason for my conception? Am I destined, purposed, called to do something great in life? Is it something that nobody else has done, something that nobody else can do but me? My brother can't do it, my sister can't do it, my husband can't do it, my wife can't do it, my pastor can't do it. Is it something so unique to my personality, so connected to my life experiences, so relative to my sphere of influence, so dependent upon my color and culture, so necessary to my needs and failures and shortcomings that nobody—no one—can do it exactly the way You want it done but me?* God's response: "Yes! You're absolutely right!"

Know that *"to whom much is given, much will be required"* (see Luke 12:48 NKJV). So get ready for the fire!

DECLARING THE END FROM THE BEGINNING

Remember this—fix it in your mind and take it to heart:

> *Remember the former things, those of long ago; I am God and there is no other; I am God and there is none like me. I make known the end from the beginning, from ancient*

times, what is still to come. I say: My purpose will stand, and I will do all that I please (Isaiah 46:9-10 NIV).

Wait a minute, God said He is declaring the end from the beginning. That's backward. That's out of sequence. That's out of order. You never declare the end from the beginning. Anybody who tells a good joke will tell you not to tell the punch line before the introduction. But God says, "I'll do it backward for you. I declare the end from the beginning. I don't start at the foundation. I reverse the order. I start with the end of it, then I go back and start working on the beginning and make the beginning work into the end." God says, "I establish purpose and then I build procedure."

POWER

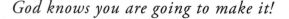

God knows you are going to make it!

LIVING

God says, "I put the victory in the heavenlies, then I start from the earth and move upward. I make sure everything is set according to My design, then I work it out according to My purpose and My plan, My will and My way." That's why God is not nervous when you are nervous, because He has set your end from the beginning. While you're struggling, groping and growling, trying to get it together, and wondering whether you will make it, God knows you're going to make it, because He has already set your end!

A friend of mine once told me how movies are made. I thought the directors shot the movie scenes in numerical sequence, beginning with the first scene and ending with the last. That is not how it is done. Most times they will shoot the final scene of the movie first. They shoot the last scene first, then roll back the film and start shooting from the beginning, making the beginning work its way into the ending.

BUILT FOR A HABITATION FOR GOD

> *Now therefore ye are no more strangers and foreigners, but fellow citizens with the saints, and of the household of God; and are built upon the foundation of the apostles and prophets, Jesus Christ Himself being the chief corner stone; in whom all the building fitly framed together groweth unto an holy temple in the Lord: in whom ye also are builded together for an habitation of God through the Spirit* (Ephesians 2:19-22).

God's approach to destiny is first establishing the purpose, then reverting to the beginning to develop you and instruct you on how to fulfill the purpose. God works out purpose the way you would design and construct a house. If you want to build a massive house, you must first hire an architect. The architect takes the vision you have for the house and transfers it onto paper (a blueprint), establishing what it shall be before it is ever built. Then the carpenter comes in and makes the vision a reality by constructing in material form (manifesting in the present) the design (vision) that the architect has established on paper (the blueprint).

Anything that is worth having is worth fighting for and worth working hard for.

Whenever the builder is confused, he refers back to the blueprint. By looking at the blueprint, he knows whether to order steel beams or wood beams, carpet or tile, brick or stucco. Whenever the builder is unclear about any detail or specification, all he needs to do is check the blueprint and look back at what the architect has declared in the design.

I want you to know that God is the Master Architect (designer) and Master Builder all in one. He never gets confused about what is planned or how it is to be built. When God builds something, He builds it for maximum efficiency and optimal performance. We get confused and doubt the outcome. Discouraged, we often find ourselves asking God, "Why did You make me wait while other people go forth? Why does it take so long for my breakthrough to come?" God responds, "What does the blueprint say? What do the specifications call for?"

Many times we wonder why we go through so much persecution. Why do we experience so much rejection that we often feel alienated by those around us just because we love God and want to do His will? God says, "I'm building a solid foundation so you'll better understand pressure and be able to go through the storms of life without being moved or shaken." God's response is simple. Anything that is made well is made slowly. "Quality must go in before the name goes on." Anything that is worth having is worth fighting for and worth working hard for.

We also have to know that God is not just building any kind of house. God is building a house of glory, a house filled with His Spirit, governed by His Word (will), and submitted to the Lordship of His Son, Jesus Christ. As tenants of that house, we are called to represent the Builder and Lord of that house by manifesting His glory on the earth. God says, "When I get through with you, when I get through nailing on you, when I get through hooking your two-by-fours together and putting windows in, when I get through hanging siding on you and placing bricks on your frame, then you are going to be a glorious edifice, a sight for the world to see." Still the house is not for us to be glorified, but that God might be exalted and glorified. *"We have this treasure in earthen vessels, that the excellency of the power may be of God, and not of us"* (2 Cor. 4:7).

VISION (REVELATION) AND PURPOSE

> *Where there is no revelation* [vision]*, the people cast off restraint* [perish]*; but blessed is he who keeps the law* [the Word of God] (Proverbs 29:18 NIV).

Solomon declared in the Book of Proverbs that where there is no vision (no divine and fresh revelation from God), the people perish (they lose control and cast off restraint).

If you are a person without direction, purpose, meaning, or understanding of God's specific intent for your life, it could very well mean that you lack vision. You may lack a personal revelation, which is God's divine insight into the reason for your being and the reason for your living. Vision not only gives meaning and understanding of one's purpose in life, it also gives you wisdom about how to bring it to pass. Vision gives understanding and reveals meaning to the trials you may experience at any given time.

POWER

Be a person of vision.

LIVING

God imparts to you a revelation of His plans for your life. That is how vision begins. Then in some cases, God confirms that word He spoke personally to you through a prophecy given to you by another man or woman of God. If you try to figure out the fulfillment of the prophecy by looking at your present situation, circumstance, or condition, it may be hard to believe without the assurance of faith and the witness of the Holy Spirit. Why would it be so hard to believe? Because when God gives you a vision, it is always too great and complex for you in your own power and ability to bring about. *"Not by might, nor by power, but by My Spirit, saith the Lord of hosts"* (Zech. 4:6).

God calls those things that are not as though they were. He calls you, in the present, what you're going to be in the future, and then makes you prove His Word to be true. Hence the Scripture says, *"...Let God be true, but every man a liar..."* (Rom. 3:4). It means you embrace what God has said about you over what everybody else has said about you, good or bad. When all has been said and done, God proves what He has said about you. It comes through His written Word and His personal revelation to you. His Word is right and everyone who speaks contrary to that Word is a liar. Your life will witness the validity of God's Word if you continue to walk by faith and obey the Father. You will prove to this world that God is real and that He is able. There is nothing else in life that pleases God the Father more.

Jesus proved the validity of God's Word when He rose from the dead. This was true regardless of the Romans, Jews, skeptics, and doomsayers who did not believe in His divinity.

My brothers and sisters, you must continue to obey and serve God. You are going to show your critics and the unbelievers that you, as the servant of God, will win in the end. Some critics will bet against you and they will speak against you. They will say, "That girl ain't never gonna be nothing. Her mama was nothing. Her aunt was nothing. I knew her grandmother and she was nothing. Her granddaddy was nothing. Her father was nothing and she is going to be nothing." According to the Word of God, *"If any man be in Christ, he is a new creature: old things are passed away; behold all things are become new"* (2 Cor. 5:17). God said that we are going to make liars out of all of them. He says, "I will remain true, and every man a liar" (see Rom. 3:4).

Some of you have been lying to yourselves, telling yourselves that you're nothing. You are telling yourself you're no good; but you ought to believe God. Believe Him in spite of your feelings or emotions. Stop believing those lying prophecies of the past—relatives and friends who claimed you would never amount to anything. Stop believing people and teachers who called you stupid. Turn a deaf ear to racism that said because you're black you are not important; sexists who said because you're a woman you're not important. Stop believing the lies. Become renewed to the truth of God. You might have had a bad childhood and have been abused, misused, rejected, and neglected. God says forget those things that are behind you and reach forth to those things that are before you. Press toward the mark of your high calling in Christ Jesus (see Phil. 3:13-14).

> ... *He is our father in the sight of God, in whom he believed—the God who gives life to the dead and calls things that are not as though they were* (Romans 4:17 NIV).

> *No longer will you be called Abram; your name will be Abraham, for I have made you a father of many nations* (Genesis 17:5 NIV).

"Calling those things that are not as though they were." The emphasis in this particular context is not on Abraham or any believer calling things that are not as though they were, but on *God* calling those things that are not as though they were. It is God, through His Word, speaking into existence

His will, not man's will. We should be very glad that it is God and not man. I wouldn't want a man to have the power to determine my future and destiny.

It is God who calls those things that are not as though they were. Our responsibility is to line up our will with His will. When we do, our lives become empowered by the grace and Spirit of God to accomplish what normally would be humanly impossible. That is the essence of authentic prophecy that comes from the heart of God.

POWER

Stop believing lies!

LIVING

If we continue to walk by faith, believing in the prophetic word that God has spoken over our lives, things that may seem impossible to realize in the natural shall come to pass.

The just shall live by faith, and anything that is not of faith is sin. For we walk by faith and not by sight (the physical senses—emotions, mental reasoning, or the things that we can visibly see). (See Romans 1:17; 14:23; Second Corinthians 5:7.) When God speaks a word into our lives, as far as He is concerned, it has already been accomplished. If the purpose has already been completed, the task or assignment has already been done; it is in essence a finished work. He calls those "things that are not as though they were."

Hebrews 10:14 declares that God offered Christ as the ultimate sacrifice for man's sin and has "...*perfected forever them that are sanctified.*" The word *perfected* in this particular passage of Scripture means in the Greek, "to bring to an end by completing or perfecting the accomplishment of bringing to completeness." This simply means that the end is already finished. It came by the supernatural power and grace given to us by what Christ accomplished during His crucifixion and resurrection.

Therefore we no longer have to strive in the flesh in order to fulfill God's purpose. The calling for our lives has already been determined in Heaven. It is a complete and finished work. Your purpose in the sight of God is already an accomplished thing, waiting for your fulfillment. *Perfected* means completely over, settled, done, and concluded. God says, "I have perfected your life and purpose. I have fixed them; I have set their course in stone. You don't have to run and see what the end is going to be." God said that it's already accomplished. The thing you're worried about performing, God said it is already done through His purpose and power.

What about all the debris in your life? What about all of those loose ends and uncertain things that Shakespeare talked about in *Macbeth?* He said, "Life is a tale told by an idiot," but God tells a different story. God says, "All of those foolish things are going to work together for the good of them who love the Lord, to them who are the called according to His purpose" (see Rom. 8:28). To walk with God, you've got to be willing to hear some things that sound foolish. Oftentimes, obeying God does seem like "a tale told by an idiot."

POWER

The thing you're worried about is already done through God's purpose and power.

LIVING

God called Moses from upon Mount Sinai and said, "Come on up here. I'm going to show you My purpose, what My plan shall be."

Moses walked upon the mountain saying, "Yes Lord, what's going on?"

The Lord said, "This is what is about to take place. There's a man down there in your church (camp) named Aaron. Aaron is to be appointed as a high priest. I'm making him an outfit: a garment symbolizing my pattern of holiness, right-eousness, and My set and divine way of communicating to My people. The outfit will have a breastplate with 12 stones, each one representing one of the 12 tribes of Israel—My chosen people. I'm getting him together, girding his loins with truth. When I get through with him, he shall be a glorious and beautiful sight for eyes to see. Aaron shall be the one who will be able to go in and out before Me." Anybody could have attempted to go in before God, but it took a holy person to come out still alive. God told Moses that when nobody else could be in His presence and live, Aaron would be anointed to come in and go out alive.

Aaron sounds like a pretty good fellow, but while God was declaring to Moses about Aaron's perfected state, He was already taking care of Aaron's end, calling those things that are not as though they were. Aaron was down at the bottom of the mountain, working on the beginning. If you were to judge from Aaron's beginning, you would not believe what was promised to this guy. As a matter of fact, the guy was down the mountain engrossed in idol worship, worshiping a golden calf. The guy just didn't have it going on. He was an idolater. He was the head of the hypocrites, president of the failures, chairman of the defeated, busy building a golden calf unto a strange god.

When Moses came down the mountain, he began to build up Aaron, exhorting him on who he was and what God called him to do and be. Moses got the revelation of the end. Moses says, "Hey man, (I'm paraphrasing), oohhh God has designed an outfit for you…. Blood, you're going to be laid out, you are going to be too sharp."

It is wonderful to have a plan, but that means nothing if you have no power to perform the plan and accomplish the purpose. God sends people in and out of your life to exercise your faith and develop your character. When they are gone, they leave you with the enriched reality that your God is with you to deliver you wherever you go! Moses died and left Joshua in charge, but God told him, "...*as I was with Moses, so I will be with thee...*" (Josh. 1:5). Joshua never would have learned that while Moses was there. You learn this kind of thing when "Moses" is gone. Power is developed in the absence of human assistance. Then we can test the limits of our resourcefulness and the magnitude of the favor of God.

I know what you probably would have said about Aaron. Something like, "Lord God, do You know where he is? Do You know what he's doing?" You don't believe God knew what he was doing? Remember, God sets the end from the beginning, calling those things that are not as though they were. God declares even to you today, as you read this book that, "In spite of what you've done, in spite of how you've failed, in spite of how you've messed up, in spite of how you have suffered, in spite of how many times you have given up and almost died, I want you to know that My grace is sufficient for you. My grace will enable you to be victorious and make it through to complete your journey (purpose). I've shed blood for you and given sacrifices for you. When I get through washing, molding, and making you into what I've already declared you are, you will show the world how glorious I am."

POWER POINTS
FOR LIVING

1. All things work together for the good of those who love God. Think of three times when God worked something good from something bad.

2. While you're struggling, groping and growling, trying to get it together, and wondering whether you will make it, God knows you're going to make it, because He has already set your end! List several ways you can keep from worrying about a situation.

3. Anything that is worth having is worth fighting for and worth working hard for. Write about something that you want that will take a lot of hard work to get. Are you willing to put forth the effort?

4. Embrace what God says about you over what everybody else says about you,

good or bad. List five things that make you special.

5. Stop believing the lies. Determine to believe the best about yourself. Write about why you will stop believing the lies people say about you—or that you say about yourself.

6. God's grace is sufficient for you. Has there been a tough time—or two—when you realized that God's grace is the only thing that got you through? Write about it.

7. Give God the glory. Thank God for ten things He has done for you today.

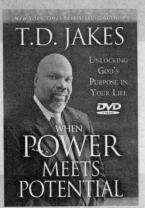

Order your copy of Bishop Jakes' new DVD *When Power Meets Potential* today at your favorite bookstore or at ChurchAlly.com and get ready to realize your God-given potential as you exercise His power in your life.

ISBN: 978-0-7684-0407-4

Price: $14.99

GET THESE OTHER GREAT TITLES FROM BISHOP JAKES

For over 20 years *Woman, Thou Art Loosed* has been helping women all over the world break free from their past and live the life God created them for. Join Bishop Jakes in celebrating 20 years of freedom with this special edition.

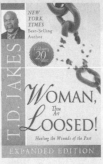

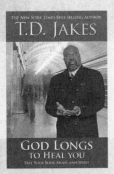

Your time for wholeness has come! Bishop Jakes uncovers the power of confession as it relates to your spiritual healing. Stop living in fear of your past and get healed of it today!

Join Bishop Jakes in this interactive devotional journal for 40 insights that will refresh and empower you to tackle life's challenges. Seek wisdom today and change your life!